ROY M. OSWALD

Making Your Church More Inviting

A
Step-by-Step
Guide for
In-Church
Training

AN ALBAN INSTITUTE PUBLICATION

The Publications Program of The Alban Institute is assisted by a grant from Trinity Church, New York City.

Library of Congress Catalog Card Number 92-72456.
ISBN 1-56699-055-6

CONTENTS

INTRODUCTION

Before You Begin

Many Christians are turned off by traditional approaches to church evangelism. The classic "Are you saved?" approach feels invasive and repulsive to most church members today. In this workbook we will explore ways church members can invite and welcome others to their church with integrity, authenticity, and ease. What natural gifts of hospitality have yet to be explored and developed? We also know that some congregations are turned off by much of the church-growth material being sold today. In this workbook we want to explore an approach to new-member outreach that fits most mainline congregations.

Over the course of three years, The Alban Institute, Inc., conducted indepth research on how congregations incorporate new members into their community life. A team of church professionals worked in Indianapolis, Philadelphia, and Atlanta with twenty-two congregations from a variety of denominations, conducting hour-long interviews with people who had joined those parishes in the last three years. We learned a lot about the way congregations assimilate new members. In each case we were able to help the congregation improve the quality of its incorporation process. The research findings from that study are written up in *The Inviting Church* (Washington, DC: The Alban Institute, 1987).

Now—here—those findings are available in workbook form. These fifteen sessions will take you through a process of reviewing your own congregation's incorporation efforts. We trust the end result will be your congregation becoming a more inviting place for visitors and potential new members. The fifteen sessions will also help participants discover gifts they have in congregational hospitality and parish outreach. This workshop design promotes a personal growth experience as well as congregational revitalization.

The workshop definitely needs a consistent facilitator for all fifteen sessions. We encourage the choice of someone who has both process and team-building skills and who has a commitment to seeing the church become a more inviting place for parish visitors.

Facilitators should read this entire workbook before the first session, so they clearly see the progression of the workshop and the gradual build up to Session 15. Some key participants may be given workbooks before Session 1, but for most participants workbooks can be distributed at the first session.

Though the pastor need not attend the sessions, we recommend that the pastor be familiar with the material and support the analyzing and brainstorming process called for throughout.

Workshop Objectives

1. To provide a personal growth experience for individuals as they explore and test their gifts at being more hospitable and inviting to parish visitors and potential new members.

2. To provide a way for a group within a congregation to assess and improve the way the congregation incorporates newcomers.

3. To systematically apply the core findings of The Alban Institute's research on the assimilation of new members.

This Workshop Is for Whom?

In the ideal setting, workshop participants would be people already serving in church leadership roles—those who serve on a committee that has a mandate to make changes in the congregation to spur numerical growth. This might be the chief decision-making body or an existing Evangelism Committee (sometimes called New-Member Outreach Committee, New-Member Development Committee, or Church Growth Committee). If this committee is small, it might invite select church members to take part in this seminar, so the group numbers ten to twelve people.

A second alternative would be to offer the class to a core *representative* group of the chief decision-making body or the Evangelism Committee, also opening the sessions to a larger group of interested church members. This way insights garnered from the class could and would be passed on to the church board or the Evangelism Committee.

A third option would be to offer the course to any interested adults, possibly as an adult Sunday school track. The drawback here is political: This group might have great ideas and plans but would have no authority to act on them. Ideas would have to be presented to church committees that, for any number of reasons, might not implement the recommendations. If this were to happen, class members might become discouraged or disgruntled.

To prevent this disheartening scenario, I recommend that you guarantee that the class include some persons on key committees, so the class has some entree into or liaison with those committees. At a minimum I recommend that the class include someone from the church council/session/vestry/consistory board, someone from the Christian Education Committee, and at least two members of the Evangelism Committee.

If your group does not have authority to implement goals and strategies, frequently acknowledge this reality and discuss strategies for presenting ideas to appropriate parties. A facilitator will need to walk a fine line—encouraging creative ideas and enthusiasm yet acknowledging that other people will need to catch the vision if programs and organizational structures are to change.

We recommend that no fewer than four or more than twelve people make a covenant to participate in these fifteen sessions. Any participants who aren't members of a standing Evangelism Committee should be given the choice at the end of the fifteen sessions as to whether or not they wish to continue carrying out the decisions of the committee. Participation should be seen as an exploratory exercise. Participants should be given the choice of deciding on follow-up work only at the end of the workshop, when goals have been clearly identified.

Class Requirements

Be up front about requirements for class participants. The covenant with individuals or the group should be:

- To attend fifteen two-hour sessions.
- To complete assigned homework readings and the surveys required for some sessions.
- To interview one or more new church members.
- To make one brief home call on a parish visitor.
- To invite one friend or family member to a worship service.
- To engage in goal setting related to helping the parish become a more welcoming church to visitors and other religious seekers.

All of these activities will be conducted within the supportive community formed for this workshop. Participants will not be asked to do something they feel they cannot do with authenticity and integrity. Facilitators will offer training and support prior to each activity.

Personal Growth

The personal growth dimensions of the sessions take three forms:

Centering

Each session begins with some centering and meditation, with each meditation relating to the subject matter of that session. As a devotional activity, centering certainly falls into an introverted spirituality category. Why use an introverted form of devotional life when the work of evangelism is usually taken on by extraverts? For two reasons. First, the introverts I meet in congregations want their churches to grow numerically. As you open a session by feeding the introverted side of your participants, they will more readily get on with the tasks of outreach to newcomers. Second, many extraverts eventually come to value a more introverted spirituality. What better time and place to introduce them to this quiet reflection?

I see the practice of centering as a way of allowing people to let go of all the baggage they brought with them to a workshop session. Centering allows people to focus in on themselves for a few minutes. Here's the general outline: Generally I ask people to close their eyes and look at the interior landscape of their lives. I encourage them to take deep breaths to help them relax physically. I explain that we relax best when the chest, neck, and head are in a straight line, when feet are flat on the floor and hands and arms fall loosely on the lap.

As I encourage them to loosen up areas of tension in their bodies, I invite them to become aware of the predominant feelings rumbling around inside them. They need not do anything with those feelings, just note that they are there and that they affect their participation in the learning event. I also ask them to become aware of their self-image at the moment. Once again, I do not ask them to change that self-image, simply to become aware of and curious about it.

After I have encouraged this heightened awareness of their bodies, feelings, and self-image, I invite them to become aware of any baggage they have brought with them to the seminar: maybe concerns heavy on their hearts, responsibilities left uncompleted. Since they can do nothing about these concerns at the moment, I invite them to package them up and send them to God. I suggest they take a few seconds to offer up a silent prayer, unburdening themselves for the duration of the session. I invite them to give themselves the gift of being totally present at the workshop, being open to fellow participants and the content of the session.

Finally, I invite them to try to view themselves through the eyes of God—with eyes of Grace. I remind them that, regardless of what feelings they have had rumbling about inside or their self-image, at this very moment God absolutely delights in their being. They are unique in the universe, and God holds their specialness close to God's heart. In God's omnipresence, God has eyes only for them. Through their baptism, they are connected to this God for eternity; there is absolutely nothing that can separate them from the love of God. I invite them to sit for a few moments and become aware of how good it feels to do absolutely nothing except enjoy the peace of God.

After all of the above, when they feel that their bodies are relaxed, that their breathing is easy, long, and deep, that they are grounded in Grace, I ask them to take their time, slowly opening their eyes. At this point we move on to the remainder of the agenda for the session.

If this type of devotional opening seems too radical a departure from what participants are used to, I suggest you open with something more familiar to them, maybe a brief Scripture reading, some silence, and a simple prayer. I would not recommend skipping over a devotional opening, as I hold some convictions about how difficult it is for people to enter immediately into the content of a workshop without having some help in making the transition from their work-a-day world.

You will note that the "Centering" sections of each session are written as a script for you to read—the "you" referring to participants, not facilitators.

Team Building

Interpersonal team building at the beginning of nearly every session allows participants to see the deeper dimensions of one another's lives. This team-building time also allows individuals to connect on a more personal level before focusing on broader concerns for the congregation's health.

Selected Sessions on Personal Growth

We in mainline denominations do little verbal "witnessing." It simply isn't our style. The outreach tasks of welcoming strangers to our congregation or inviting friends and family members to attend church with us is going to feel awkward. Exploring these activities provides personal growth experiences as well as congregational revitalization. Sessions 1, 9, 10, and 11 have a more personal than corporate focus. The remaining sessions engage participants in some sort of congregational analysis, always exploring ways in which the parish might become more inviting. Let's begin.

Building the Team

Facilitator: Before the Session, arrange chairs in a large circle.

Centering

"I invite you to close your eyes for a moment of quiet reflection. Find a comfortable position—feet flat on the floor, head, neck, back aligned. Sitting straight. Hands set loosely on your lap. From this quiet place, I invite you to become aware of the feelings you bring to this first session. Do you bring feelings of hope—both for yourself and your congregation? *(Pause.)* Do you bring negative feelings about the workshop? Is there something you fear or dread? *(Pause.)* You don't need to do anything about these feelings. Simply note their existence and that they affect your approach to the session.

"I now invite you to focus on your feelings about the people who have decided to take this course with you. Entering the room and seeing who was in the group, what did it feel like? Which people do you want to get to know better? Which people give you some concern? Know that God can bring healing between you and someone else in this room. Take a moment and say a prayer, asking for that healing. *(Pause.)*

"I invite you now to become aware of your body. Are you holding tension anywhere? Breathe deeply in, out. With each exhale, feel yourself letting go of a piece of that tension.

"Now focus on the holy Mysterious One who hovers in our midst, for wherever two or three are gathered together in Jesus' name, there he is in the center. Turn your thoughts to gratitude—for the Spirit being active in your life, for all the ways you are blessed by God. *(Pause.)* Allow the Spirit to open your heart to any call to help our congregation become a more inviting place for others.

"When you are ready, when you are breathing easy, long, and deep, when you are relaxed and grounded in Grace, slowly open your eyes. Then we'll continue with the session."

Workshop Introduction

Especially if your group is not a standing committee with authority to make and carry out decisions, introduce the workshop as an exploratory event; you've gathered to brainstorm ideas and envision possibilities. Even if your group does have decision-making power, make it clear that priorities for goal setting won't be sorted out until Session 15, when you sit down and look at the total picture, analyzing what you've learned in all previous sessions. Until then, your group is opening doors to possibilities—asking what if we tried this, what if we tried that? This exciting exploratory work lays the groundwork for subsequent decisions. The decisions themselves won't be made in the workshop.

Team Building and Class Activity

To learn, grow, and work together effectively we first need to build a team. Members of dynamic teams generally know each other well and have developed a sense of trust. They also have clear leadership and know what to expect of their leaders.

Here, let's work on the trust issue. Without trust it is difficult for a person to learn and grow. Trust is an important element in a personal transformation. In short, personal growth calls for a type of vulnerability, a willingness to explore areas of pain, fear, or confusion. Very few people want to be vulnerable with others they don't know or trust. That's why it's so important to begin these sessions by giving serious attention to the team-building effort. The group needs to get to know one another well, so they feel comfortable entering into a potentially threatening learning situation.

Anticipating the Workshop

Begin by asking participants to risk some self-disclosure. Give each person three minutes to talk about signing up for these fifteen sessions: What excites you about this workshop? What concerns you about participating in this workshop?

Articulating One's Faith

Give each participant five minutes to answer a second round of questions concerning personal habits related to talking about personal faith and being members of this parish: To what extent do you feel good about how you articulate to others the deeper meaning of your life, especially how you relate to God? How or where do you feel inadequate in the way you verbalize your faith? To what extent do you talk to others, especially non-members, about how much this parish means to you? After you have gone around the circle and everyone has shared, allow for a ten-minute general discussion on these issues.

Desiring Church Growth

The last set of questions focuses on members' desires for their church to grow numerically. Ask individuals if they want this church to grow numerically; if so, why? By how much? You might list on newsprint reasons people give for wanting the church to grow.

Let's assume the majority of participants claims to want this church to gain new members. Launch into a general discussion about the cost such growth will demand of the parish.

Parishioners often say they want their church to grow numerically but are out of touch with the personal and corporate cost of such growth. It is folly to think that, for example, a congregation of three hundred members could add another fifty new members without those newcomers changing that congregation in significant ways. Growth usually entails some sacrifice on the part of long-time members. Are members of the parish ready and willing to make the sacrifices necessary for numerical growth to take place? What will such growth cost the congregation? What changes and sacrifices would growth demand?

It's important to list responses on newsprint. Once such a list is complete, the group can assess the extent to which those costs are realistic given their growth goals. Once that assessment has taken place, draw the discussion to a close: Do you still want to grow numerically? Are you willing to pay the price?

We will return to this last question following Session 2, when we have more clear data about the ministry dynamics of congregations of various sizes and the costs of moving from one size congregation to another. For now, you have plenty to work with in this opening session.

Homework Assignment

Announce that before the next session, participants should read the "Class Assignment" on pages 5-13.

Closing

Close with a minute of silence to reflect on the insights gained in the proceedings. Then have someone close with a simple prayer of blessing.

SESSION TWO

Changing Sizes of Congregations

Class Assignment:
How to Minister Effectively in Family, Pastoral, Program, and Corporate Size Churches

In the following article, addressed to clergy and written for The Alban Institute's bimonthly journal, *Action Information*, I focus on the difficulty congregations have as they grow and require a new style of pastoral leadership. Between Sessions 1 and 2, participants should read the article and make some assessment as to what description best suits their congregation.

The theory of congregational size that I find most workable is Arlin Rothauge's, described in his booklet *Sizing Up a Congregation for New Member Ministry* (The Episcopal Church Center, New York, NY 10017; $3 plus $2 postage and handling). It was originally written to help congregations recognize the different ways different-sized churches assimilate new members. When a theory is on target, however, it so accurately reflects reality that it can be applied to other dimensions of a church's life and work. Rothauge's theory elicits consistent "ahas" from clergy who are reflecting on their transition from one size parish to another. Whether churches are growing or downsizing, congregations hold on to deeply engrained assumptions about what constitutes a dynamic church and what effective clergy do. The inflexibility of these expectations is an important cause of clergy malfunctioning.

Rothauge sets forth four basic congregational sizes. Each size requires a specific cluster of behaviors from its clergy. The average number of people attending weekly worship and the amount of money being contributed regularly provide the most accurate gauge of church size. Since membership rolls fluctuate wildly depending on how frequently they are evaluated, they cannot provide an accurate measurement of congregational size. Rothauge also holds that a church's size category is a matter of attitude as much as numbers. I knew of one congregation that averaged 700 at Sunday worship and still functioned on a Pastoral model. All the pastor did was preach on Sunday and visit people through the week. The pastor's perception of his job burned him out and eventually cost him his marriage and his ministry.

Here is a brief description of each of Rothauge's four sizes and my understanding of what members expect of clergy in each size.

The Patriarchal/Matriarchal Church: Up to Fifty Active Members

This small church can also be called a Family Church because it functions like a family, with appropriate parental figures. The patriarchs and matriarchs control the church's leadership needs. What Family Churches want from clergy is pastoral care, period. For clergy to assume that they are also the chief executive officer and the resident religious authority is to make a serious blunder. The key role of the patriarch or matriarch is to see that clergy do not take the congregation off on a new direction of ministry. Clergy are to be the chaplain of this small family. When clergy don't understand this, they are likely to head into a direct confrontation with the parental figure. It is generally suicide for clergy to get caught in a showdown with the patriarchs and matriarchs within the first five years of their ministry in that place.

Clergy should not assume, however, that they have no role beyond pastoral care. In addition to providing quality worship and home/hospital visitation, clergy can play an important role as consultants to these patriarchs or matriarchs, befriending these parental figures and working alongside them, yet recognizing that when these parental figures decide against an idea, it's finished.

Clergy should watch out for the trap set when members complain to them about the patriarch or matriarch of the parish and encourage the pastor to take the parental figure on. Clergy who respond to such mutinous bids, expecting the congregation to back them in the showdown, betray their misunderstanding of the dynamics of small-church ministry. The high turnover of clergy in these parishes has taught members that in the long run they have to live with old Mr. Schwartz who runs the feedmill even when they don't like him. Hence it is far too risky for members to get caught siding with pastors who come and go against their resident patriarch/matriarch.

Because these congregations usually cannot pay clergy an acceptable salary, many clergy see them as stepping stones to more rewarding opportunities. It is not unusual for a congregation of this size to list five successive clergy for every ten years of congregational life. As Lyle Schaller claims, the longer the pastorates the more powerful clergy become. The shorter the pastorates the more powerful laity become. These Family Churches have to develop one or two strong lay leaders at the center of their life. How else would they manage their ongoing existence through those long vacancies and through the short pastorates of the ineffective clergy who are often sent their way?

The president of The Alban Institute, Loren Mead, began his ministry in a Family Church in South Carolina. Later in his ministry he attended a clergy conference at which he discovered seven other clergy who had also started their ordained ministry in the same parish. As they talked, those clergy realized that, in view of the difference in their styles and the shortness of their tenures, the only way that parish survived was to take none of them seriously.

One of the worst places to go right out of seminary is to a Patriarchal/Matriarchal Church. Seminarians are up to their eyeballs in new theories and good ideas. They want to see if any of them work. Even though some of those good ideas might be the ticket to their small church's long-term growth and development, the church's openness to trying any of them is next to zero. Sometimes, through the sheer force of personal persuasion, a pastor will talk a congregation into trying a new program or two. Pretty soon parishioners find themselves coming to church events much more than they really need to or want to. As they begin then to withdraw their investment from these new programs, the clergy inevitably take it personally. Concluding that their gifts for ministry are not really valued in this place, they begin to seek a call elsewhere. On the way out of the church they give it a kick, letting the parish know in subtle ways that they are a miserable example of Christian community.

These small congregations have endured such recriminations for decades. The message they get from their executive is that they are a failure because they fail to grow while consuming inordinant amounts of time. Middle judicatories try to merge them, yoke them, close them—mostly to no avail. You can't kill these congregations with a stick. Large churches are far more vulnerable. An exec can place an incompetent pastor in a large church and lose 200 members in one year. Yet the same exec can throw incompetent clergy at Family Churches, leave them vacant for years, ignore them—all with little effect. The Family Church has learned to survive by relying on its own internal leadership.

These congregations need a pastor to stay and love them over at least ten years. This pastor would have to play by the rules and defer to the patriarch's or matriarch's leadership decisions for the first three to five years. At about year four or five, when the pastor did not leave, the congregation might find itself in somewhat of a crisis. At some level they would be saying, "What do you mean you are going to stay? No clergy stay here. There must be something the matter with you." Then the questioning might begin: "Can we really trust you? Naw! You are going to leave us like all the rest." In this questioning we can see the pain of these congregations. For a minute, let's put ourselves in their shoes and imagine an ordained leader walking out on us every few years, berating us on the way out. Would we invest in the next pastor who came to us? Not likely! It would be simply too painful. The Family Church may have invested in one five years ago, only to find that the pastor left just when things started to move. Basically these people have learned not to trust clergy who repeatedly abandon ship when they see no evidence of church growth.

I conclude that we need to refrain from sending these congregations seminary trained pastors. History demonstrates that these churches have not been served well by full-time ordained clergy. The Episcopal Diocese of Nevada and the North Indiana Conference of the United Methodist Church are among judicatories experimenting with employing persons indigenous to the communities, providing them with some basic training to give long-term pastoral care on a part-time basis. I believe long-term tent-making ministries offer the best possibility for ministering to many of these Patriarchal/Matriarchal Churches.

If denominations and middle judicatories persist in placing newly ordained clergy in these parishes, they should do so only after laying out this theory for these clergy, helping them discover who indeed are the patriarchs and matriarchs of the parish, suggesting some strategies for working with them. If these clergy find it simply too difficult to work with these parental figures, they need to let their executive know promptly. Rather than leaving these newly ordained clergy regretting that they pursued ordained ministry in the first place, the exec should move them out of the Family Church.

The Pastoral Church: 50 to 150 Active Members

Clergy are usually at the center of a Pastoral Church. There are so many parental figures around that they need someone at the center to manage them. A leadership circle, made up of the pastor and a small cadre of lay leaders, replaces the patriarchs and matriarchs of the Family Church. The power and effectiveness of the leadership circle depends upon good communication with the congregation and the ability of the pastor to delegate authority, assign responsibility, and recognize the accomplishments of others. Without such skill, the central pastoral function weakens the entire structure. The clergyperson becomes overworked, isolated, and exhausted, may be attacked by other leaders, and finally the harmony of the fellowship circle degenerates.

A key feature of a Pastoral Church is that lay persons experience having their spiritual needs met through their personal relationship with a seminary trained person. In a Pastoral Church it would be rare for a Bible study or a prayer group to meet without the pastor. The pastor is also readily available in times of personal need and crisis. If a parishioner called the pastor and indicated that she needed some personal attention, the pastor would drop over to see her, probably that afternoon but certainly within the week —a qualitatively different experience from being told that the first available appointment to see the pastor in her office is two weeks from now. The time demands on the pastor of a Pastoral Church can become oppressive, however, most members will respond with loyalty to a reasonable level of attention and guidance from this central figure.

A second feature of the Pastoral Church is its sense of itself as a family where everyone knows everyone else. If you show up at church with your daughter Julie by the hand, everyone will greet you and Julie, too. When congregations begin to have 130 to 150 people coming every Sunday morning, they begin to get nervous. As Carl Dudley put it in *Unique Dynamics of the Small Church* (Washington, DC: The Alban Institute, 1977) they begin to feel "stuffed." Members wonder about the new faces they don't know— people who don't know *them*. Are they beginning to lose the intimate fellowship they prize so highly?

Clergy also begin to feel stressed when they have more than 150 active members whom they try to know in depth. In fact, this is one of the reasons why clergy may keep the Pastoral Church from growing to the next larger size congregation—the Program Church. If clergy have the idea firmly fixed in their head that they are ineffective as a pastor unless they can relate in a profound and personal way with every member of the parish, then 150 active members (plus perhaps an even larger number of inactive members) is about all one person can manage.

There are some clergy who function at their highest level of effectiveness in the Pastoral Church. Given the different clusters of skills required for other sizes of congregations, some clergy should consider spending their entire career in this size congregation. Since the Pastoral Church can offer a pastor a decent salary, clergy do tend to stick around longer. If clergy can regard themselves as successful only when they become pastor of a large congregation, then sixty-five percent of mainline Protestant clergy are going to end their careers with feelings of failure. Two-thirds of mainline Protestant congregations are either Family or Pastoral Churches.

Clergy with strong interpersonal skills fare well in the Pastoral Church. These clergy can feed continually on the richness of direct involvement in the highs and lows of people's lives. Clergy who enjoy being at the center of most activities also do well. There are lots of opportunities to preach and lead in worship and to serve as primary instructors in many class settings for both young and old. Outgoing, expressive people seem to be the best matches for the style of ministry in the Pastoral Church. An open, interactive leadership style also seems to suit this size church best.

Growth in the Pastoral Church will depend mainly on the popularity and effectiveness of the pastor. People join the church because they like the interaction between pastor and people. When new people visit the congregation for the first time, it is likely to be the pastor who will make the follow-up house call.

When a congregation grows to the point where its pastor's time and energy is drawn off into many other activities and the one-on-one pastoral relationship begins to suffer, it may hire additional staff to handle these new functions so the pastor can once again have plenty of time for interpersonal caring. Unfortunately, this strategy will have limited success. To begin with, when you hire additional staff you then have a multiple staff, which requires staff meetings, supervision, delegation, evaluation, and planning. These activities draw the pastor deeper into administration. Then, too, additional staff members tend to specialize in such things as Christian education, youth ministry, evangelism, or stewardship, which tends to add to the administrative role of the head of staff rather than freeing his or her time up for pastoral care.

As we move to the next size congregation, notice the change in the diagram of the church's structure. Clergy consider a congregation's transition from Pastoral to Program size the most difficult. One can expect enormous resistance on the part of a Pastoral Church as it flirts with becoming a Program Church. Many churches make an unconscious choice not to make the transition and keep hovering around the level of 150 active members. The two treasured features of a Pastoral Church that will be lost if it becomes a Program Church are ready access to their religious leader and the feeling of oneness as a church family, where everyone knows everyone else and the church can function as a single cell community.

Two things can prevent a congregation from making that transition: The first barrier is found in the clergy. When clergy hold on to a need to be connected in depth to all the active members, they become the bottlenecks to growth. The second barrier is found in the lay leaders who are unwilling to have many of their spiritual needs met by anyone except their ordained leader.

It is most helpful to put this theory up on newsprint before the chief decision-making body of the church and ask where it thinks the parish stands. If they have been saying "yes, yes" to church growth with their lips, but "no, no" with their behavior, this theory can bring their resistance to the conscious level by pointing out the real costs they will face in growing. Churches tend to grow when parish leaders, fully aware of the cost of growth, make a conscious decision to proceed.

Without the backing of key lay leaders, the cost of moving from a Pastoral to a Program Church usually comes out of the pastor's hide. The parish may welcome the pastor's efforts in parish program development, while still expecting all the parish calling and one-on-one work to continue at the same high level as before. Burnout and/or a forced pastoral termination can result.

The Program Church: 150 to 350 Active Members

The Program Church grows out of the necessity for a high-quality personal relationship with the pastor to be supplemented by other avenues of spiritual feeding. Programs must now begin to fill that role.

The well-functioning Program Church has many cells of activity, which are headed up by lay leaders. These lay leaders, in addition to providing structure and guidance for these cells, also take on some pastoral functions. The Stewardship Committee gathers for its monthly meeting and the committee chair asks about a missing member. Upon being told that Mary Steward's daughter had to be taken to the hospital for an emergency operation, the chair will allow time for expressions of concern for Mary and her daughter. The chair may include both of them in an opening prayer. If the teacher of an adult class notices that someone in the class is feeling depressed, the teacher will often take the class member aside and inquire about his well-being. Even if the teacher eventually asks the pastor to intervene, the pastor has already gotten a lot of assistance from this lay leader.

Clergy are still at the center of the Program Church, but their role has shifted dramatically. Much of their time and attention must be spent in planning with other lay leaders to ensure the highest quality programs. The pastor must spend a lot of time recruiting people to head up these smaller ministries, training, supervising, and evaluating them, and seeing to it that their morale remains high. In essence the pastor must often step back from direct ministry with people to coordinate and support volunteers who offer this ministry. Unless the pastor gives high priority to the spiritual and pastoral needs of lay leaders, those programs will suffer.

To be sure, a member can expect a hospital or home call from the pastor when personal crisis or illness strikes. But members had better not expect this pastor to have a lot of time to drink coffee in people's kitchens. To see the pastor about a parish matter, they will probably have to make an appointment at the church office several weeks in advance.

When clergy move from a Pastoral Church to a Program Church, unless they are able to shift from a primarily interpersonal mode to a program planning and development mode, they will experience tension and difficulty in their new congregation. It is not that clergy will have no further need for their interpersonal skills. Far from it—they need to depend on them even more. But now those interpersonal skills will be placed at the service of the parish program.

Key skills for effective ministry in a program church begin with the ability to pull together the diverse elements of the parish into a mission statement. Helping the parish arrive at a consensus about its direction is essential. Next the pastor must be able to lead the parish toward attaining the goals that arise out of that consensus. In the Program Church, clergy need to be able to stand firm at the center of that consensus. To wilt in the face of opposition to this consensus will be seen as a lack of leadership ability. The Program Church pastor will also need to be able to motivate the most capable lay persons in the parish to take on key components of the parish vision and help make it become a reality. Developing the trust and loyalty of these parish leaders and ensuring their continued spiritual growth and development is another key part of the cluster of skills needed in the Program Church.

For clergy who get their primary kicks out of direct pastoral care work, ministry in a Program Church may leave them with a chronic feeling of flatness and lack of fulfillment. Unless these clergy can learn to derive satisfaction from the work of pastoral administration, they should think twice about accepting a call to this size parish.

The Corporate Church: 350 or More Active Members

The quality of Sunday morning worship is the first thing you usually notice in a Corporate Church. Because these churches usually have abundant resources, they will usually have the finest organ and one of the best choirs in town. A lot of work goes into making Sunday worship a rich experience. The head of staff usually spends more time than other clergy preparing for preaching and worship leadership.

In very large Corporate Churches the head of staff may not even remember the names of many parishioners. When members are in the hospital it is almost taken for granted that they will be visited by an associate or assistant pastor, rather than the senior pastor. Those who value highly the corporate church experience are willing to sacrifice a personal connection with the senior pastor in favor of the Corporate Church's variety and quality of program offerings.

Sometimes the head pastor is so prominent that the personage of the pastor acquires a legendary quality, especially in the course of a long pastorate. Few may know this person well, but the role does not require it. The head pastor becomes a symbol of unity and stability in a very complicated congregational life.

The Corporate Church is distinguished from the Program Church by its complexity and diversity. The patriarchs and matriarchs return, but now as the governing boards who formally, not just informally, control the church's life and future. Laity lead on many levels, and the Corporate Church provides opportunity to move up the ladder of influence.

Key to the success of the Corporate Church is the multiple staff and its ability to manage the diversity of its ministries in a collegial manner. Maintaining energy and momentum in a Corporate Church is very difficult when there is division within the parish staff. Any inability to work together harmoniously is especially evident during Sunday worship where any tensions among the ordained leadership of the parish will manifest themselves in subtle ways.

It is at this point that clergy making the transition to the Corporate Church find themselves most vulnerable and unsupported. Our denominational systems do little to equip clergy to work collegially within a multiple staff. A three-day workshop on the multiple staff is a bare introduction. Leaders in industry with master's degrees in personnel management still make serious mistakes in hiring and developing leaders for the corporation. The head of staff of a Corporate Church learns to manage a multiple staff by trial and error. Sacrificing a few associate and assistant clergy on the altar of experience is the price the church pays for such lack of training.

For the most part clergy are not taught to work collegially. In seminary we compete with one another for grades. Each of us retreats to his or her own cubicle to write term papers. There is little interaction in class. In seminary we don't really have to take each other seriously. This might change if, for example, a professor were to assign four seminarians to complete research on a church doctrine, write one paper, and receive a group grade. In that kind of learning atmosphere we would have to take one another on and argue about our different theological perspectives and forms of piety. Unless our training can begin to equip us for collegial ministry, our seminaries will continue to turn out lone rangers who don't really have to work with other clergy until they get to the Corporate Church or the larger Program Church. By that time our patterns have been set.

The clergy who are called as head of staff in Corporate Churches are usually multi-skilled people who have proven their skill in a great variety of pastoral situations. In a multiple staff, however, the senior minister will need to delegate some of those pastoral tasks to other full-time staff members, who will inevitably want to do them differently. Learning to allow these people to do things their own way is in itself a major new demand.

Our research with the Myers-Briggs Type Indicator shows that congregations are best served when the multiple staff includes different types. The more diverse the staff, the greater its ability to minister to a diverse congregation. But this requirement for diversity makes multiple staff functioning more complicated: The more diverse the staff, the harder it is to understand and support one another's ministries.

Lay leaders are generally completely baffled by the inability of ordained people to work collegially. "If our religious leaders aren't able to get along, what hope is there for this world?" they may wonder. Lay leaders could help enormously by seeing to it that there is money in the budget for regular consultative help for the staff. This help is not needed only when tensions arise. Multiple staffs need to be meeting regularly with an outside consultant to keep lines of communication open and difficulties surfaced.

When the multiple staff is having fun working well together, this graceful colleague-ship becomes contagious throughout the Corporate Church. Lay people want to get on board and enjoy the camaraderie. The parish has little difficulty filling the many volunteer jobs needed to run a Corporate Church.

In addition to learning to manage a multiple staff, clergy making the transition to head of staff need to hone their administrative skills. These clergy are becoming chief executive officers of substantive operations. Yet I would emphasize leadership skills over management skills. While managers can manage the energy of a parish, leaders can *generate* energy. The Corporate Church needs leaders who know how to build momentum. Otherwise, even when managed well, these large churches run out of gas and begin to decline.

In summary, the most difficult transitions in size are from Pastoral to Program or, when downsizing, from Program to Pastoral. These are two very different ways to be church. More is required than a theoretical vision of the shift. We need to deal with the fact that a shift in size at this level just doesn't feel right to people. Somewhere deep inside they begin to sense that it doesn't feel like church anymore.

[end of homework]

Centering

"Let's go inside once again and be quiet with ourselves. What things do you notice when you take the opportunity to focus completely on yourself? What primary sensations are you receiving from your body? *(Pause.)* What feelings seem to dominate your life at the moment? *(Pause.)* Let's also be grounded in our sexuality. How are you feeling about yourself as a woman or a man?

"Let's also become aware of another reality present with us. Right now God is raining down upon us an abundance of Grace. Here in this room there is more Grace than any of us can use. Let's relax into it. If we are open to it, this Grace relaxes and heals every place it touches. Breathe in this Grace and allow it to touch all the hurting places in your life. If you are hurting physically, breathe in this Grace and allow it to go directly to that spot to work its powers. If you are hurting emotionally, allow this Grace to penetrate your soul and transform that part of your life. Let's be quiet for just a moment in the presence of this Grace.

"Now imagine yourself going back in time to visit the church of your childhood. If you remember several churches, pick the one that had the greatest impact on you. If you did not attend church, did you ever attend a church wedding, a baptism? Think of that congregation. Envision yourself as a child seated in a pew in that church on a Sunday morning. What images return to you as you revisit that church? See if you can look around and estimate how many people are with you in that church. *(Pause.)* Besides Sunday worship, recall some favorite memories of your life with the people in that congregation.

"Return to an awareness of your breathing. Check once again to see that your body is relaxed. When you are ready, slowly open your eyes, then we will continue with the rest of this session."

Team Building

Give everyone in the group one minute to describe the size of the childhood congregation envisioned in the centering exercise. Share a few important memories of that church. It's important to hold this team-building exercise to fifteen minutes, so each member needs to be brief. It is surprising how much one can say in sixty seconds.

Class Activity

It is not uncommon for parishioners to want to add a hundred new members to the parish but be unwilling to change one thing about their parish to accommodate the increase. We often refer to this as the vampire theory of growth: "We need some new blood around here." Basically members desire a bunch of new people to help pay the bills and to fill up the choir, Sunday school, and sanctuary, but they don't expect to make any sacrifices related to the things they want from their church.

Some of the greatest upheaval caused by numerical growth occurs when a congregation is on the borderline between two of the four different sizes of congregations described in the assigned reading. When a parish crosses the boundary between one size and another, it needs to begin relating to its clergy in fairly radically different ways than previously. As a review of the assigned reading, ask four participants to volunteer, each to summarize the dynamics of one of the four types of congregations. At the end of each summary ask the group if it remembers any additional points. Fill in any important aspects not brought up. Briefly discuss what description best suits your parish.

Remind the group that the most difficult transitions are between the Pastoral and Program Churches. The following activity will help illustrate what a transition from one size church to the other might mean.

Ask participants to stand and push the chairs to the side of the room, clearing the floor.

Rather than have participants simply circle answers to prepared questions, I like to send the "A's" to one side of the room and the "B's" to the other side. You can see at a glance where everyone stands on an issue, and the two groups can talk to each other about their choices. Since the questions deal with choices clergy need to make between two competing activities, I ask any clergy present to remain silent until the other participants have answered.

Have one side of the room represent response A and the other side represent response B. Read aloud one set of A-B choices. Have participants choose their responses by going to the designated side of the room. Tally the results. Allow up to two minutes for the two groups to discuss their stance, then go on to the next question.

Choice Points for Clergy

Each set of questions represents a choice point for your pastor. Should your pastor have had a week full of crises and only limited time left, which response represents your preference for what the pastor should do?

A. Visit more shut-ins?
B. Prepare a better sermon?

A. Attend a wedding reception?
B. Go on a retreat with parish staff?

A. Call on prospective members?
B. Conduct a training session for church officers?

A. Visit a bereaved family?
B. Help two church officers resolve a conflict?

A. Make a hospital call on a fringe member?
B. Attend a continuing education event?

A. Give pastoral counseling to members?
B. Attend a planning event with officers?

A. Call on parishioners?
B. Recruit leaders for parish events?

A. Attend an activity with parish youth?
B. Critique a meeting with a church officer?

Once you have completed the exercise as a class, invite the pastor to share personal responses to each question. I encourage clergy to choose the activity they would most enjoy rather than the one they believe might claim a higher parish priority. The differences between the pastoral and lay responses to these questions may result in some fruitful discussion related to size of congregation and pastoral expectations.

As a follow-up to this activity, ask various participants to volunteer to read aloud (a paragraph each) the following "Class Reading."

Class Reading

This activity can point out several issues:

1. Congregations may be Program size yet still require their clergy to attend to all the category A pastoral activities. This is a perfect prescription for burnout. It can also

lead to labeling clergy as "bad" because they don't accomplish all the tasks in the A column while they are also expected to crank out quality programs for the parish (Category B activities).

2. Clergy in small Pastoral Churches should be focusing their energies and attention on the A activities. But sometimes because their background or training is in Program Churches, they continue to concentrate on the B activities or feel guilty because they aren't doing so.

3. Clergy and laity often disagree on priorities for clergy. This exercise often surfaces those differences quickly and makes role negotiation possible.

Staffing for Growth

Some congregations do not grow because they are not staffed for growth. If, for example, you are a Program Church, expecting your pastor to assist you in developing and executing quality programs in the church, yet you also expect your pastor to do pastoral calling in homes, you probably have a pastor who is doing neither task well and is burning out trying to do it all. Unless those pastoral expectations change or you add more staff, the congregation will not grow, as members are going to be dissatisfied with both the programs that are offered and the fact that they are not receiving the pastoral care they desire.

As a rule of thumb, if you desire to staff for growth, you need one full-time program person on your staff for every one hundred active members. (This does not include support staff such as janitors or secretaries.) *Active members* refers to how many are attending worship on the average year round. You are staffing for maintenance if you are just slightly under that figure. You are staffed for decline if you are seriously under that figure.

Growing churches see that their members as well as their visitors receive adequate pastoral care during times of crisis or need. People well cared for pastorally are inclined to invite their friends and family members to become affiliated with their parish. When a new family to your area is having difficulty, having a staff member make a call to discover ways the parish can meet needs makes a deep impression. Without that call, they are less likely to think of joining your congregation.

The addition of a paid professional, i.e., youth worker, religious education specialist, business manager, usually pays for itself within twelve to eighteen months. For example, a congregation with 225 active members that hires a third full-time staff member to provide better quality ministry will most likely grow to 300 members.

Class Discussion

1. Again consider the question of whether or not your church wants to grow numerically, considering this additional information about the costs involved.

2. From your perspective, is your congregation not growing numerically because the size of your congregation is out of sync with the expectation you are placing on the pastoral staff? Your responses to the previous exercise should give you some clues here. Spend no more than fifteen minutes discussing this question.

3. Does your congregation need to look into creative alternatives for meeting the pastoral needs of your members and newcomers? Possibilities might include:

   a. Hiring a retired pastor to visit shut-ins, hospitalized members, and others in pastoral need. (It is not that your pastor would cease all visitation, but make visits shorter and less frequent.)

   b. Organizing and training lay volunteers to do pastoral work, including calling and informal counseling. Stephen Ministries (1325 Boland, St. Louis, MO 63117) offers a comprehensive volunteer training program you might want to consider.

   c. Adding one or more part-time persons to your program staff to raise the quality of programs offered to members and newcomers, i.e., director of education, director of youth ministry, director of children's choir, building manager, director of outreach and evangelism. These program specialists would free your pastor to have more time to tend to the congregation's pastoral needs.

Spend no more than thirty minutes exploring some of these alternatives.

4. Consider the current size of your congregation and your goals for growth. Discuss your congregation's staff needs. Are you staffed for growth, maintenance, or decline? What if any additional staffing would you recommend to your chief decision-making body? Urge participants to write down goals in the "Notes" section that follows. Save these goals for reference in Session 15.

Closing

Close the session with a few moments of silence and a brief prayer.

Notes

Goals for easing the transitions of church growth:

_____
_____
_____
_____
_____
_____
_____
_____
_____
_____
_____
_____
_____
_____
_____
_____
_____
_____
_____
_____
_____
_____
_____
_____
_____
_____
_____
_____
_____
_____
_____
_____

The Wisdom of Newcomers

Facilitator: Before the Session, photocopy the questionnaire on pages 21-26, one copy for each newcomer your participants will interview between Sessions 3 and 4. From the church office obtain a list of names, addresses, and phone numbers of people who have joined the parish in the last three years. Get two names for each workshop participant, plus a few extra, in case interviews can't be arranged.

Centering

"Let's begin again by quieting ourselves. Breathe deeply in, out. Relax. Let the tension of the day fall away. Psalm 68:6 says that God places the solitary in families. Think of one caring community God has placed you within. *(Pause.)* Recall a second community, maybe one in your past. Community is one of the many ways God manifests Grace in concrete form.

"Recall your first visit to or memory of our parish here. What did it smell like? Sound like? What were the first things that caught your eyes? What did you feel? Can you recall whom you first talked to upon entering the church? The content of those first conversations? What was your first impression of the pastor? What were your first impressions of the worship experience? What images of God began to emerge for you as a result of worshipping with this congregation? Did your belief systems change as a result of your affiliation with this congregation? If so, how would you describe this shift in your theology? In this congregation were you fed spiritually in a different way than in former congregations, if there were former congregations? In what ways do you feel well fed spiritually in this parish? What spiritual needs have gone unmet?

"Once you have finished this brief reverie, focus again on your body and breathing. When you are ready, slowly open your eyes."

Team Building

Have each participant take one minute to answer these questions: What spiritual needs are being well met in this parish? In what areas do you still experience some spiritual hunger?

Class Activity

Introduce this activity with these brief comments: In initial research on the incorporation of new members, The Alban Institute contracted with twenty-two congregations to interview all newcomers who had joined the parishes in the last three years. Through those interviews The Institute gained most of the insights presented in the book *The Inviting Church*. What's more, those twenty-two parishes learned a great deal about themselves —their strengths and weaknesses—from the reports of the interviewers. Each report presented a congregation with an opportunity to ease a person's transition from being an outsider to an effective member in the parish. In most cases participating congregations were surprised to see how difficult they had been making it for persons to feel as if they were integral parts of those congregations.

Through this study the researchers came to prize the wisdom of newcomers. At the end of the study they concluded that they could do an effective analysis of any congregation simply by interviewing its newcomers. It is uncanny how someone new to a congregation knows things about that parish that consistently eludes the old timers.

You also can tap into the inherent wisdom of those who have joined your parish. But to prepare your group for interviewing newcomers, let participants learn from one another, as they recall visiting this parish for the first time.

Have participants pair up with a person they don't know well. Have each pair find a quiet corner. Using the following questionnaire, have each take twenty minutes to interview the other, asking about his or her entry experience. Regardless of how long ago it was, everyone will have memories of early encounters with your parish. Any clergy attending this workshop should be interviewed as well, as the way a congregation incorporates new members is very similar to the way it incorporates a new pastor. Interviewers should write summaries of the answers they receive in the appropriate spaces on the questionnaire. A time keeper should indicate when the paired partners should reverse roles at the end of twenty minutes. Assure any participants who do not finish the questionnaires that getting the interview practice was more important than answering every question.

Incorporation of New Members Questionnaire

I. Awareness

A. How did you learn about this church?

B. What things originally attracted you to this parish?

C. What were you looking for in a church family or worshipping community?

D. When you first came, were you singled out or identified as a newcomer? How?

E. Was there anything that almost kept you from becoming active in this congregation? If so, what?

F. As a newcomer what were your first impressions of this congregation?

G. How much time passed between the time you started attending and the time you decided to join?

___Several weeks ___Six months ___One year ___More than a year

H. Did you transfer your membership from another church to this one?

__Yes __No

If so, what was the most difficult part for you in transferring membership?

II. Hospitality

A. What people helped you move deeper into the life of the parish?
Give names or positions.

B. When did you feel accepted in this congregation?

1. Immediately upon your first visit?
2. When you joined?
3. During a class?
4. Still don't feel accepted?
5. Other?

C. When did you get a membership directory?

__Immediately __Upon joining __Do not have one
__Within one month __Three months __Six months __One year

D. When and in what context did you have your first conversation with the pastor?

E. Did a lay person or lay team visit you in your home after you began attending? __Yes __No
If so, how long after your first visit to the parish?

Did the clergy visit you? __Yes __No
If so, how long after your first visit to the parish?

F. What if any surprises did you experience while getting acquainted with this congregation?

G. Describe any changes that have taken place in your life since becoming active in this congregation.

H. Has any experience involved with the church made you feel uncomfortable, awkward, or put off? What happened?

I. Describe the most moving or satisfying personal experience you've had in this parish.

III. Response

A. Besides Sunday worship, in what church programs or activities did you first become active?

B. How did you become involved in your first activity?

__ Personal initiative __ Invitation by parish staff __ Invitation by friend
__ Other

C. What does the parish do to make its programs and activities known and available to newcomers?

D. How were you made aware of financial responsibilities to this parish?

E. Has the congregation communicated to you what it expects of its members?
    __ Yes __No
    Briefly describe your understanding of any expectations.

F. Did the congregation offer to train you to recruit other potential members?
    __Yes __No
    If so, what did they offer?

G. Did the church train you for any other outreach ministry?
    ___Yes __No
    If so, what ministry? What training did they give?

IV. Going Deeper

A. How important is Sunday worship in your expectations of a church?

1	2	3	4	5	6

    Unimportant   Very important

    Rate this parish in its ability to meet your worship needs.

1	2	3	4	5	6

    Unable   Very able

B. In what ways does this parish function differently from others you have known?

C. How are differences or conflicts managed within this congregation?

D. What image does this church try to project to its members and those outside the church?

E. Did the parish invite you as a newcomer to take on any personal spiritual discipline of your own? __Yes __No If so, what?

F. Has the congregation gathered information on your interests and abilities to assist you in moving deeper into the life of the parish?
__Yes __No
If yes, how have they followed up with such assistance?

In what ways might the church do this work more effectively?

G. Have you noticed any conscious efforts of the parish to help newcomers and old timers get to know each other better? __Yes __No
If so, what?

Note to Interviewer:
"Is there anything else that I didn't ask about your experience of joining?
Thank you very much."

Additional Notes:

_____
_____
_____
_____
_____
_____
_____
_____
_____
_____
_____
_____
_____
_____
_____
_____
_____
_____
_____
_____
_____
_____
_____
_____
_____
_____
_____
_____
_____
_____

Debriefing

Have newsprint, markers, and masking tape available. Have participants return to the large group and ask what they learned about themselves and their parish through the one-on-one interviews. Once individuals have been able to share both their positive and negative experiences as they recall their own incorporation, elicit some generalizations that arise about the way this parish goes about that task. Where does your congregation do a good job in welcoming visitors and inviting them to go deeper into the life of the parish? What potential stumbling blocks were identified?

Encourage participants to make note of these generalizations in the "Notes" section at the end of this session.

Preparation for Newcomer Interviews

With the time that remains, try to nail down how each participant will carry out one or two interviews with people who have joined the parish in the last three years. Have available a listing of these people, their addresses, and phone numbers. Also pass out photocopies of the questionnaire, so each interview is conducted on a clean sheet. Have each person covenant to conduct one or two of these interviews between now and the next session, by telephone, by arranging to meet the newcomers at the church, or by visiting their homes. This is "homework" for the next session. Participants are to bring completed questionnaires to Session 4.

Referring participants to the questionnaire, point out the "Additional Notes" space at the end of the last page. Here interviewers can make notes *after* leaving the interviews. What personal characteristics might be of interest and affect the way this person was welcomed: age, race, demeanor, appearance, verbal skills, and so forth?

Take time to calm people's fears about interviewing newcomers. In our original research we discovered that newcomers loved to be debriefed on their experiences. Many had not reflected much on the experience and welcomed the opportunity to talk about it. Interviews not only provide information, but in the process they also create much good will in the parish. Through this activity you are communicating to newcomers that the parish really cares about their being welcomed.

Encourage participants to remain impartial and objective throughout these interviews. If newcomers have had some negative experiences in the parish, interviewers should not defend the parish or try to fix anything. Simply hearing the person out is a ministry in itself. Remind interviewers to ask for candor in the beginning of the interviews, and thank newcomers for it at the end.

Option

Depending on how many persons are in the workshop and how many newcomers come to the parish, another option would be to identify a few recent visitors to the congregation who did not decide to affiliate or join. When you contact such persons by telephone, they are usually quite candid about why they did not continue attendance. Their reasons may have little to do with what your parish had to offer and more to do with their own personal needs. On the other hand, their decision may have had something to do with barriers in your incorporation process of which you are not aware. You will learn a lot from these interviews; it will be worth your while to contact some of these people (again, obtain addresses from the church office) and have one or two participants interview them.

Closing

Once all the ground work has been laid for these interviews between now and the next session, have someone close with a simple prayer.

Notes

Generalizations seen as a result of our own experiences as newcomers to this parish:

_____

_____

_____

_____

_____

_____

_____

_____

_____

_____

_____

_____

_____

_____

_____

_____

_____

_____

_____

_____

_____

_____

_____

_____

_____

_____

_____

_____

_____

_____

Notes continued . . .

Listening to Our Newcomers

Centering

"Let's again focus in on ourselves. Close your eyes. Place your feet flat on the floor. Hands in your lap. What stress is your body carrying? Where is that stress sitting in your body? Breathe deeply, in, out. Imagine that stressed limb, neck, back, loosening up. Focus in on your feelings. Name them. Acknowledge their presence. Focus in on your relationship with the Holy Mysterious One who floods us daily with Grace upon Grace upon Grace. Rest for a few moments on that deep sense of peace that can permeate your body and psyche as you reflect on God's Mercy and Grace. When you are ready, focus again on your body, your breathing. Slowly open your eyes."

Team Building

Have each participant take one minute to tell the group about the high and low point of the day. If the group is meeting in the morning, ask about the high and low point of the week.

Class Activity

The purpose of this session is to have participants relate their experiences of interviewing one or more newcomers and to identify ways in which your parish can improve the way it incorporates newcomers into its midst.

1. Debriefing. If the group is larger than six, divide into small groups of three or four. Ask each group to listen to each person's experience of interviewing newcomers to the parish. Allow each person to speak five minutes for each interview conducted.

2. Listing learnings. Once everyone has summarized the interviews, the small group should list on newsprint what it learned from one another's reports. This is like a brainstorm list, with all observations of the group being placed on the newsprint. What is your church doing right? What is your church doing wrong? Take no more than ten minutes for this activity.

3. Prioritizing and goal setting. Gather the groups together and have each small group report its list of learnings. Refer also to the notes you made in Session 3—what the group learned about the church from its own entry experience.

Following some general discussion of these positive and negative points, have the group prioritize its learning so that no more than three or four key insights are listed on one newsprint sheet titled: Obstacles Our Church Presents to Newcomers. Then brainstorm ways the parish might make the incorporation process into the parish smoother and easier. What changes might the parish need to make to prevent persons from stubbing their toes as they enter into membership in this parish? How might you become a more "inviting church"?

Once three or four changes have been identified (as goals), record them—in the "Notes" section at the end of this session—for future reference. (As facilitator, you should keep this newsprint "short list.") As you accumulate goals in each session, this group or another decision-making body will need to decide which are the most important to address in the next twelve months. More on that later.

You might end the session on a positive chord by listing two things the parish is doing right in terms of welcoming newcomers. Note that you want to make a conscious effort to continue these practices.

Closing

Close with a brief moment of silence and a simple prayer.

Notes

Goals for making this parish a more inviting church:

_____

_____

_____

_____

_____

_____

_____

_____

_____

_____

_____

_____

_____

_____

_____

_____

_____

_____

_____

_____

_____

_____

_____

_____

_____

_____

Notes continued . . .

The History That Is Our Journey

Centering

"Let us be quiet in the peace of God. Close your eyes for a moment and look inside yourself. We're told that the peace of God passes human understanding. Relax into that wonderful peace that comes from being connected through baptism to the One who will never allow us to be separated from God's eternal caring. *(Pause.)*

"Now shift your focus to feelings, your feelings about this congregation. Recall some great moment you have had in the parish. Maybe a second great moment. Recall a time when you needed something special from the parish and how someone came through for you.

"If by some incredible catastrophe the parish were wiped out by a fire or a bomb, what would you miss most about the place? Whom in the parish would you miss the most? What customs and rituals unique to this place could not be replaced by another worshipping community? Take a moment to thank God for all that is special to you about this congregation.

"When you are ready, focus again on your body. When you are breathing easy, long, and deep, when your body is totally relaxed, when you are grounded in Grace, slowly open your eyes to continue with the session."

Team Building and Class Activity

Virtually all of Session 5 is a team-building activity focusing on the history of your parish. Begin the activity with these introductory notes:

The purpose of this historical reflection and discussion is to help participants become aware of the spiritual journey of the parish and the special strengths and liabilities that come with the parish culture. The history of a congregation carries enormous weight, like a person's genetic code. The momentum of a congregation's history is so powerful that it will continue into the future on a given path unless a majority of members makes a conscious, intentional decision for it to be otherwise. Most of the time congregational members are unaware of that path they're on, only that "this is the way things are always done around here."

This is not to say that all the momentum of a congregation's history is bad. Most congregations have many positive things going for them in their history. One positive goal of this historical reflection is to isolate and highlight all the things about your congregation's history that you want to preserve and continue to live out.

But there is another reason for this activity. No congregation can escape having some negative history that keeps repeating itself. At The Alban Institute we call it "coming to terms with your history." A congregation that does not own up to its negative side will forever be condemned to repeat that side of its life.

In short, the advantage of a congregation periodically discussing its history is to place onto the table (consciousness) what was formerly under the table (unconscious), giving the group an opportunity to make a conscious decision about some of the revealed insights. Here and now we're going to look at the church's patterns of numerical growth and some of the things that have spurred that growth. This activity will give you a better idea of the strengths of the parish that can be incorporated into your appeal to nonchurch members. It can also put you in touch with some of the destructive patterns of the parish that continue to turn away potential members.

Recording Your History

For this activity you will need a wall on which you can post up to twenty feet of newsprint. On the far right of that newsprint write the word *present*. At the far left print the words *congregation's beginning*. Since most congregations recall their history by pastorate, print each successive pastor's name (and date—year—of pastoral transition) from left to right along the top of the newsprint. Along the bottom of the newsprint, place occasional historical events to remind people of that era, i.e., end of World War II, the year Kennedy was shot, the end of the Vietnam War.

Gather your group around the newsprint and ask a different participant to act as scribe for each pastorate. Beginning in the present and working backward, ask participants to recollect the most important events that took place in each pastorate. You'll want to complete this historical time line in forty-five minutes, so budget your time well. Continue to press for contributions to the time line, as everyone will be tempted to stop and discuss incidents. Once you have all the significant historical events of one pastorate, move on to the next. As you move further and further back in your history, you may reach the point where no one present remembers a pastorate. At that point simply put down stories or incidents related by others.

Events recorded might include: building programs, starting (or discontinuing) a study series or outreach ministry, new staff members, "trouble with" staff members, instituting new curriculum, deaths, disasters, and so forth.

Complete this portion of the activity without referring to written records. For now, what actually happened is less important than what people think happened. Here you're uncovering the myths about yourself by which you live. What you think happened is more a part of the myth than what actually took place.

What you have before you now is a gold mine of information. You have a record of the most important historical events of your parish as perceived by the people in the room. Depending on how you feel about sharing your perceptions with others in the congregation, you might post the string of newsprint in a prominent place within the church. Place a sign above the newsprint inviting people to add to or disagree with the historical reflection. You might also involve the congregation at a deeper level by setting aside an evening of historical reflection, repeating this exercise with a broader constituency. Connect it with a pot luck dinner and make a fun evening of it. In my experience this has always proved to be an enjoyable activity, as people relish getting in touch with their past. Inevitably people, including some of the old timers, will say, "I didn't know that about us." The newcomers will be fascinated with the spiritual journey of the congregation they have joined.

Meaning Statements

Continue your historical reflection by developing "meaning statements" from observations made as you reflect on the whole history of the parish. Invite participants to answer the question, What does our history mean? If you have invited other members of the parish to join you for this exercise or if you have more than eight in your workshop, you might divide the group into teams of four and have each group write on newsprint any generalizations they see as they review the history of the parish. Two groups usually generate more observations than one.

Generalizations should include both positive and negative statements; some might seem completely "off the wall." That's okay. Later on the group will select and focus on statements that have the greatest meaning to everyone. For now you want to develop as long a list of observations as you can.

Have participants open their workbooks to the following "Sample List of Meaning Statements." You might go around the room, asking each person to read one statement.

Sample List of Meaning Statements

Food seems important to us around here. We love our pot luck dinners.

Whenever we engage in a building program, we seem to get a new spurt of energy.

We seem to be hard on associate pastors. Three of the last four associates have left under a cloud.

There never seems to have been a time when we weren't fussing over something. It almost seems as if we get our energy from our little internal squabbles.

Up until the last ten years this parish has always reached out to the immediate neighborhood in some caring fashion. I wonder if our struggle with numerical growth has to do with our having stopped that practice.

This congregation seems to thrive when we are getting strong leadership from our clergy, and we go into a slump when we aren't getting this.

It seems as though strong preaching has never been something we require of our clergy. We do insist, however, that they love people.

This congregation has never had a big stewardship effort. I wonder if our consistent lack of money is tied to this.

This parish always seems to place a high priority on our ministry to children. I think it is one of our strengths.

In all our talk about being diverse and racially inclusive, we have yet to receive a person of color into membership.

We have always shied away from conflict. It feels as if our conflict avoidance behavior is a main source of difficulty.

It appears as if the women have carried this congregation in the last twelve years. Also, we have had no specifically men's activities in the last ten years. What has happened to our men and men's programming?

This congregation grew steadily until 1967. Since then we have been on a steady decline. That is also when we stopped fifty-fifty giving to our national church. I wonder if there is a connection.

Since we've gone to multiple services and added a separate educational hour on Sunday morning, our numerical growth has climbed steadily.

It wasn't until Millie Jo took it upon herself to stand out in front of the church every Sunday morning and welcome strangers that we had any type of outreach to parish visitors.

In our history we have had two periods when our parish staff did not get along. In both cases we experienced a decline in attendance.

This parish has always relied on a strong lay leader to keep its energy up. When we don't have one, we seem to sink into a black hole.

Two of our last four clergy have gone through divorces while serving this parish. Are we hard on clergy marriages?

The life of this parish centers around music. Is this what makes us different and special?

It appears that this parish has always preferred a casual, informal worship setting. Whenever we've had clergy who try to shape us up liturgically, there has been rebellion.

Spend thirty minutes in small groups, writing down meaning statements for your parish.

Prioritizing

Have participants return to the large group. Ask a spokesperson from each group to report the group's list. As a second or third group reports, cross out and consolidate statements that repeat the basic point of a previously given observation. As a group, work together to choose the most important positive and negative generalizations about the congregation. Important negative statements would be those that the congregation must confront if it is to become healthier and increase its opportunities for growth of any kind. Important positive statements would point out qualities so central to the life of the parish that you would be foolish to abandon them; parish life would not be the same without these attributes. In one sense the exercise of historical reflection is a type of long-range planning activity, isolating qualities that need to continue—or change—if this place is to have a viable future.

To prioritize statements, you might number each meaning statement and give each person in the room three votes for what he or she identifies as the three most important observations, positive or negative. Go around the room and tally the results, i.e., Mary Lou would say, "I vote for numbers 4, 12, and 18." Place a star next to those statements, then ask the next person to vote. Or you might go down through the list and have people raise their hands to indicate their votes.

You can quickly isolate the top priorities of the group. I would recommend that you not identify more than five or six priorities, as a congregation or committee can handle only so many. In fact, three would be more manageable.

Action Plan

End the session by turning these top priorities into goal statements. If the meaning statement is a positive one, the goal statement should focus on how the parish might capitalize on that strength. For example, music has always been a strength of this parish; we propose getting this message out to the community in the following ways . . .

For negative meaning statements, goals should focus on ways the parish can move beyond that damaging dimension. Ask a participant to read aloud the following examples.

Class Reading

Children's Ministry

This parish has never been a very welcoming place for children. *(If presenting this as a report to a decision-making body, you might want to list various observations that led to this negative conclusion.)* To attract younger couples to our church, we might do the following:

a. Plan and publicize a special activity for children once a month from September through May.

b. Once a quarter center a Sunday worship service on children.
Feature the children's choir. A Sunday school class might put on a brief biblical drama. Emphasize children sitting with their parents that Sunday. Maybe ask three adolescents to stand up and introduce their parents and say three things they value about them.

Handling Conflict

Our congregation's indirect way of dealing with conflict encourages gossip and sniping and drains people's energy for projects. To counter this we might:

a. Suggest a six-Sunday adult forum on healthy ways of dealing with conflict.

b. Develop recommended ground rules to follow when someone hears gossip or negative comments about another member of the parish. The ground rules would recommend that the person making negative remarks deal directly with the aggrieving person.

c. Suggest that the pastor preach a series on the positive side of conflict--how we might use conflict as a way of building positive energy in the parish. How did various biblical characters deal with conflict in constructive ways?

Class Activity Wrap-Up

If you don't have enough time in this session to flesh out goal statements related to one or more top-priority meaning statements, shelve this portion of the activity until Session 15 when you will pull together goals for the entire seminar.

Homework Assignment

Before the next session, participants should read the "Class Assignment" that starts on page 43 and goes to page 45.

Closing

Close the session with some silence and a brief prayer relating to insights discovered in this session.

Notes

Top priority meaning statements and related goals for being a more inviting church:

_____

_____

_____

_____

_____

_____

_____

_____

_____

_____

_____

_____

_____

_____

_____

_____

_____

_____

_____

_____

_____

_____

_____

_____

_____

_____

_____

Norms—Discovering the Rules by Which We Live

Class Assignment

Before Session 6, participants should read the section "Norms: Every Church Has Them."

Norms: Every Church Has Them

Norms are those unwritten psychological rules that govern behavior in any human community. Norms are generally unconscious and are least available to old timers in the parish. Long-time members of a community eventually become unaware of the subtle ways they change their behavior when relating to others in that community. When people enter their parents' home, they simply behave differently than they do when they enter a shopping mall or their favorite restaurant.

Newcomers to a parish are most conscious of parish norms. When they attend congregational activities they become aware of the norms of your parish; they usually expect them to be similar to the norms of a former parish, maybe the one in which they were raised.

Many newcomers get hit in the face by "surprise" expectations or norms. Their immediate—though unvoiced—question usually is, "Why are you doing it that way?" Worse yet, they may feel anger or disgust: "These people and their 'rules' are so backward or uncaring." Uncovering these reactions is a key benefit of your having interviewed newcomers to your parish. Possibly you have already learned from the "wisdom of newcomers."

Once norms become known to a parish, it can make a conscious choice to change or alter destructive norms while enhancing and emphasizing the positive. For example, a norm within a large, wealthy, downtown church we studied was this: During the coffee hour, held in a large, well-appointed room with tables for four, it was perfectly all right for members to play catch-up with their friends while strangers stood alone on the sidelines, coffee cups in hand. The church had done this for years. It was almost like a "hazing" that newcomers had to endure if they wanted to become members of the parish. For years this parish touted many members on the "who's who?" list of the city's socialites.

When asked, newcomers said that to join the church you had to run the gauntlet of humiliation and embarrassment. At one time people had been willing to fight their way because they wanted to belong to this prestigious church. Unfortunately, both its reputation and its membership had seriously declined in the past ten years; that norm was going to have to change if the church was going to have a run at reversing the trend.

The roots of each parish norm can be found some place in the congregation's history. Having just come through your historical reflections in Session 5, you have completed the ground work for uncovering both the positive and negative norms of your parish. At the end of Session 6 you will be invited once again to develop goals—goals that will capitalize on your positive norms and/or alter or minimize destructive norms.

For me, the most important goals a congregation can adopt are those that deal with norms. Whenever I am invited by a congregation to consult on their goal-setting process, I inevitably find a group ready to set goals akin to those in a corporate setting: Let's raise our budget by ten percent, repair our roof, upgrade our organ, and add fifty new members to our Sunday school. I see these as secondary goals. These goals do not address the root issues that de-energize our people and make our religious community less attractive for both insiders and outsiders. A congregation that is able to surface hidden norms and develop a set of goals that (1) addresses the most destructive norms and (2) capitalizes on the most attractive and positive norms, is working on core issues. Though these goals may be hard to surface and address, the payoff for successfully developing them will be long-term.

If a church-growth program is to have some depth, it needs to get beyond mere gimmicks that grease the skids as newcomers move toward membership. From my perspective, two things need to be happening simultaneously. Yes, you need to deepen the sense of welcome extended to parish visitors. A thoughtful follow-up needs to be in place. With some clarity the newcomer needs to hear about requirements for membership. These aspects deal directly with the incorporation process.

As congregations are trying to clean up their acts on the incorporation process, they also need to be raising the quality of life within the parish. Once newcomers are assimilated into the parish, is there anything of quality to offer them? Stated another way, parish visitors will be able to forgive some foibles in the incorporation process if they perceive that they are joining a quality community, with good news preached regularly by both clergy and laity, a community with values and a way of serving others that is congruent with what it says about itself. This is a group that walks its talk.

It's similar to what is important in a restaurant. To be sure, people need to be warmly received when they enter; the decor needs to be pleasant; the service superior. Yet in the final analysis, the quality of the food is going to bring people back for more— or keep them away. I have come to call this "strength at the center." Without some strength at the center, the slickest incorporation process is bound to fail in the end. People need to be offered substance along with a congenial process.

Every parish has unwritten rules related to:

1. Children—how they are viewed and treated; what behavior is expected of children and parents.

2. Men/Women—how they are treated the same or differently; what behavior is expected of men that is different from that expected of women. Some expectations are positive and some are negative.

3. Conflict—how differences of opinion are dealt with or resolved; what confrontational behavior is expected; whom you can disagree with and whom you can't.

4. Money—amounts people are expected to give; how money is managed and spent; which efforts have higher priority than others.

5. Treatment of clergy—how clergy are addressed; how well they are paid; what behavior is expected of them; where they are not expected to be taken seriously, how parishioners have a right to abuse them.

6. Newcomers—who talks to them; what behavior is expected of them; what limits are placed on their power; to what extent their foibles are forgiven; which kinds of people are more acceptable in this parish than others.

I could list additional categories of unwritten rules. I have identified these six, as I think they are most important in a review of a parish's incorporation process.

[end of homework]

Centering

"Again I invite you to close your eyes, relax your body. Breathe deeply, exhaling the tensions of the day. Peel off your work and home concerns as if they were a bulky coat you didn't need indoors. Focus on the unbelievable Grace of God. Consider why you are here, concerned about welcoming people to the church: because you have drunk deeply from God's bottomless cup of love. Because you—we—have been healed by the touch of God, we want others to taste that Grace and return for more.

"Reflect on what makes this church different from any other church you have known. Imagine yourself sailing a half mile above the congregation. Let's say the roof is off the church. You can look down and observe all the Sunday morning interactions of the parish. Then you observe activities throughout the week. Do you notice how people's behavior changes, just subtly, the moment they step foot inside the church? *(Pause.)* Every existing human system is run by unwritten rules that govern behavior within those systems. What positive and life-enhancing rules do the people in our parish live by?

(Pause.) What negative and life-diminishing rules? (Pause.) Picture yourself walking into the church. How does your behavior change when you step foot inside the door? How is your behavior different at church than in your work setting? How is your language different? Your dress?

"Now focus again on your breath. When you feel your body relaxed, slowly open your eyes."

Team Building

Give participants one minute each to talk about (1) a custom (norm) of the parish that continues to throw them off balance or (2) a custom they have never quite gotten used to.

Class Activity

Briefly review the homework assignment, asking participants to describe the six listed categories of parish norms.

Discovering Our Norms

Divide participants into groups of three. Give each small group several sheets of newsprint. Depending on your workshop size, assign each trio one or more of the six categories of parish norms, so that all six are "taken." Give the groups sixty minutes to put on newsprint their "hunch" as to the norms of the parish in their assigned categories. The first reaction of most participants will be, "We don't have any unwritten rules related to children; this is crazy." Simply insist that they try their best to identify their sense of any norms. Whenever I have facilitated this exercise with a parish, skeptical groups emerge with three or four items in a category. Everyone sits there with mouth open, saying, "That's right. Those are rules we live by around here."

Explain that unwritten rules might—or might not—look similar to meaning statements. If what is discovered in this session echoes findings of Session 5, all the more reason for the group to continue to plow that turf; the issues are obviously important.

Ask one person in each group to serve as a time keeper, dividing the sixty minutes among the assigned categories. People will be surprised by all the things that can surface even in twenty or thirty minutes when they focus attention and give their intuitions free rein.

Following the hour of small-group work, call the large group together. Have each group tape its newsprint to the wall and report on its conclusions in each assigned category. At the end of each report, invite participants to offer feedback. Do they sense the validity of each stated norm? Do they see others to add to the list? Cross off the lists any items that do not receive the support of most of the large group. Once all the groups have made reports, take a magic marker and number all the norms remaining on all six lists.

Setting Goals

Invite the group to prioritize the agreed-upon parish norms. Which three to five are deemed most important in terms of the parish's state of health?

In one sense, the healthier you become as a parish, the more draw you will have for newcomers. You become the kind of religious community that outsiders seek.

Once again, give participants three votes as they choose the most important norms to be addressed if the congregation is to move to greater health. Through the simple tally process used in Session 5, determine the top three to five norms.

For the remainder of the session, have participants list some possible goals that address the three top-priority norms. How can unhealthy norms be minimized? How can healthy norms be accentuated? Suggestion: Since Sessions 3, 4, and 7 center on welcoming newcomers and Session 8 focuses on children's ministry, you might confine this goal-setting exercise to top-priority norms in four categories: men/women, conflict, money, treatment of clergy.

Be sure to keep the top-rated norms and any related goals for further consideration in later sessions. Encourage participants to write this critical information in the "Notes" section below, for their own reference.

Homework Assignment

Ask that participants read the "Class Assignment" on workbook pages 49-52 before Session 7. Make a special point of noting the request that participants spend ten minutes watching pedestrians in a shopping mall setting to determine who would be welcome in your church.

Closing

End the session with a moment of silence and a brief prayer of guidance for the parish.

Notes

High priority norms this parish needs to address and related goals:

_____

_____

_____

_____

_____

_____

_____

_____

_____

_____

_____

_____

_____

_____

_____

_____

_____

_____

_____

_____

_____

_____

_____

_____

_____

_____

_____

_____

_____

_____

SESSION SEVEN

Parish Norms—
Who Is Welcome in Our Congregation?

Class Assignment

Before Session 7, participants should read the following article, "Who Is Welcome in Our Congregation?"

Who Is Welcome in Our Congregation?

Every congregation has unwritten rules about who is welcome in its midst. On a planning retreat, whenever I ask a congregation, "Who is welcome in this place?" the inevitable answer is "Everyone." At that point I say, "I'm sorry, not everyone is welcome here. You may try to be cordial to everyone who steps foot inside the door, but that does not mean everyone is welcome."

Unfortunately, most congregations are unaware of their discrimination of parish visitors. In our initial research on the assimilation of new members who had joined a congregation in the last three years, we noted conflicting data. I recall interviewing one newcomer who told me what a wonderful, warm, and friendly congregation this was. Several interviews later, a person described the same congregation as being cold and uninviting. What made the difference? You simply had to look at these people to know the difference. One was a well-dressed, educated, articulate male; the second was a woman with probably no more than a high-school education; she was struggling economically and not well dressed.

Some people are going to slip into your church like a hot knife into butter. Others are going to struggle with whether or not they are really accepted by you.

Before next class, for fun, sit for ten minutes in a shopping mall and watch people walk by. As you note specific individuals coming toward you, make a subjective judgment: Would this person receive a warm welcome in our church? You might be surprised at the number of people you identify as being less than welcome.

An ultimate goal of every parish should be to become so heterogeneous that it offers a genuine warm welcome to all shapes, sizes, races, and sexual orientations, regardless of their dress, history, or cleanliness. There is no question about God's love of them. Each is a unique child of God; there is a special ache in God's heart for each of them. Someday we may mature to the point where we are able to love them as God loves them. In the meantime we need to work at this, becoming more heterogeneous one step at a time.

I disagree with much of the church growth literature that says if you want to grow numerically, look at the people already attending your church; go out and invite people exactly like them. I will admit that this tack does work. You will have greater success inviting to your church carbon copies of the persons sitting in your pews. But you will increasingly become a ghetto of like-type people. This makes the 11:00 a.m.. Sunday morning worship the most segregated hour in American life. In the long run your congregation becomes less able to reach out to a heterogeneous neighborhood for membership. On the other hand, the more varied your congregation, the more able you are to reach out to the variety of persons seeking a religious community and church home.

The following list names various types of persons. By no means exhaustive, the list will help you get a clearer picture of who is really welcome in your parish. Working alone, place a rating beside each descriptive phrase, according to the following directions.

Welcome Rating

Directions: Rate each phrase in one of three ways: I for TOP; M for MIDDLE; B for BOTTOM. Persons rated TOP are those who regularly receive a sincere welcome in your parish. Persons rated MIDDLE may or may not get a warm welcome, depending on other factors. People rated BOTTOM will likely have a hard time being received openly in the parish.

___ Elderly single male
___ Elderly single female
___ Couple living together, not married
___ Interracial couple
___ Divorced male
___ Divorced female
    Non-English-speaking male
___ Non-English-speaking female
___ New Age seeker
___ Extremely overweight male
___ Extremely overweight female
___ Couple with a crying/screaming baby
    they won't leave in the nursery
___ Person with noticeable hygiene needs
___ Person who sings in a loud monotone
___ Person who sings operatically
___ Someone especially talkative
___ Someone especially quiet and meek
___ Anglo Saxon, articulate, well-educated, wealthy male
___ Anglo Saxon, articulate, well-educated, wealthy female
___ Persons who are married and attend services together
___ Inarticulate, well-dressed male
___ Inarticulate, well-dressed female
___ Caucasian low-income male
___ Caucasian low-income female
___ Aging white male with financial resources
___ Aging white female with financial resources
___ Child of middle-income parents
___ Teenager of middle-income parent
___ White male, not dressed in fashion
___ White female, not dressed in fashion
___ Male more than seventy years old
___ Female more than seventy years old
___ Single male under thirty

__ Single female under thirty
__ Unemployed male
__ Unemployed female
__ Person on welfare
__ Afro-American middle-class male
__ Afro-American middle-class female
__ Afro-American male on welfare
__ Afro-American female on welfare
__ Hispanic male
__ Hispanic female
__ Asian male
__ Asian female
__ Arabic male
__ Arabic female
__ Mildly physically disabled (needing walkers, crutches) person
__ Highly disabled (in a wheelchair) person
__ Gay male
__ Lesbian
__ Gay couple
__ Lesbian couple
__ Person with alcohol on breath
__ Person with many teeth missing
__ Emotionally disabled person (unpredictable behavior)
__ Retarded youth or child
__ Retarded adult
__ Smoker
__ Political liberal
__ Political conservative
__ Agnostic
__ Religious fundamentalist
__ Religious charismatic
__ Person with Alzheimer's disease
__ Cancer victim
__ Unmarried pregnant teenager
__ Person with dirt under fingernails and unkempt hair
__ Male wearing one earring
__ Female with tight, short skirt and a scarecrow hairdo
__ Person testing HIV positive
__ Ex-prisoner
__ Recovering sex addict
__ Person implicated in a sex scandal

Centering

"As we move to a quiet internal space to prepare ourselves for this session, let's close our eyes, relax our bodies, and turn over to God all the problems and concerns we bring to this time together.

"As you breathe in, imagine that the oxygen entering your lungs, your bloodstream is the love of God. Focus on the incredible acceptance you experience every time you turn to God and surrender the control you normally think you need to have over your life. But the unconditional positive regard God has for us is more constant and reliable than the air we breathe, even before we give over the controls of our life. Try to see yourself through the eyes of Grace. What messages does your mind send you that you don't deserve this unconditional positive regard? *(Pause.)* What barriers keep you from viewing yourself with the unconditional acceptance of God? Imagine those barriers falling down. Walk into a place where you accept yourself as God accepts you.

"Focus now on church friends, neighbors, strangers. That Scripture passage is correct: We love others as we love ourselves. If we don't accept ourselves, how can we accept others? How often do we take our dark sides, the rejected parts of ourselves, and try to project them onto others? If we see our own dark shadows in other people whom we consider evil or undesirable, we don't have to claim the shadows as our own. Think about one person you have a hard time accepting. Can you identify some dark quality in that person that might also be in you? Some dark part of yourself that you have not yet come to accept? *(Pause.)*

"As you open yourself to God's unconditional acceptance, be assured that God is faithful. Don't despair if you can take only small steps toward accepting yourself. God isn't through with any of us yet. When you are ready, focus again on your breath. When you feel totally relaxed once again, when you are breathing easy, long, and deep, slowly open your eyes."

Team Building

Give each participant one minute to describe one person—at work, in the neighborhood, or in the family—that he or she has recently had a hard time accepting. Allow this to be a type of confession. At the end of each account, have the group repeat the phrase, "God is merciful."

Class Activity

Review and summarize the homework assignment. Ask for any reports of "mall watchings." Were people surprised at their feelings or judgments?

Ask participants to turn to their "Welcome Rating" on pages 51 and 52. Working as a group, go down through the list, reaching a consensus on a profile of your church. You may reach consensus quickly on some categories and have a harder time with others. Before arriving at a group consensus, hear out each person's reasons for rating a description a certain way. You might suggest that participants write the consensus rating in the right margin, after each description.

Once you've reached consensus, suggest that the congregation could work to be more welcoming to categories in the MIDDLE range—people on the borderline between being heartily welcomed and accepted and being given an ambivalent response at best. See if your group can agree on three or four types of persons in the MIDDLE range that, with a little work, could find their way into the hearts of your members. Point out that few people are going to want to belong to a church if their presence is not desired by the majority in that parish. People often seek out a church family for the very reason of finding a community that will care for them deeply, especially when they are down and out and at their worst.

As a group also discuss whom God seems to be sending your way at this time. If the demographics of your neighborhood are changing, who is moving in? Ask the class to turn to the "Class Reading" below. Read these paragraphs aloud, as an example, to spur discussion of your own church.

Class Reading

A congregation is in a neighborhood where more apartments are being built. They determine that this means an influx of single persons, including single parents. The congregation assumes that it extends a warm welcome to singles, yet when you look seriously at who is valued most in the parish, you see that "being attached" counts. And most of the church programming assumes a traditional family unit. In this church, as in most, singles feel like fish out of water when they attend pot luck meals. The language used in Sunday morning announcements is rarely inclusive of singles. Divorce is still seen as a failure by many parishioners, making single parents generally feel like outsiders to the mainstream of parish life.

If this congregation in this type of changing neighborhood is to grow numerically, its first goal should be to open up its exclusive family orientation. It might appoint some singles to several key committees. The parish could look into offering a few programs that would more directly speak to the needs of singles. Gradually as more singles become part of parish life, the norm of who is acceptable in the parish would shift to include singles.

Activity Wrap-Up: Goal Setting

Return to your list of types of persons, focusing on those rated in the MIDDLE category. Which types of these MIDDLE people live in the neighborhood of the church? Which show some interest in your parish? What goals might your group develop to help your congregation become more inviting to these people?

Again, keep a list of these goals so you can refer to them in Session 15.

Homework Assignment

Announce that participants should read the "Class Assignment" reading on pages 57-59 of this workbook before the next session.

Closing

Take just a moment for silence before people rush out to the four winds. Then have someone conclude the silence with a brief prayer.

Notes

Goals for being more inviting to groups of people we now welcome halfheartedly:

_____

_____

_____

_____

_____

_____

_____

_____

_____

_____

_____

_____

_____

_____

_____

_____

_____

_____

_____

_____

_____

_____

_____

_____

_____

_____

_____

Being More Inviting to Children

Class Assignment

Before Session 8, participants should read the following article, "Becoming More Welcoming to Children."

Becoming More Welcoming to Children

An astounding statistic emerged in our research in response to the following question asked of newcomers in twenty-two congregations of various denominations in Indianapolis, Philadelphia, and Atlanta: *What brought you to this church?*

    2 percent—an advertisement
    6 percent—an invitation by the pastor
    6 percent—an organized evangelistic outreach program
  86 percent—an invitation by a friend or family member

There's power in the personal invitation of friends or family members! And our discovery is confirmed by other church-growth research.

The implications of this are glaringly clear. If a church wants to grow numerically, it needs to encourage and cajole its own members to invite their friends to church. The credibility of a friend or family member exceeds by a hundredfold the credibility of a stranger trying to invite someone to church.

Our research also showed that most members of mainline Protestant churches are timid at this point—more than timid; some hold deep convictions that you do not violate another person's integrity by pushing your religion on that person. They feel it is almost anathema to mention their church involvement to friends. This will be the subject of Session 9, where we will return to these statistics. In this session let's focus on children. How can we encourage children of the parish to invite their friends to Sunday school and other parish activities geared to children?

Successfully encouraging children to invite their friends to church and supporting their efforts is much easier than getting adult parishioners to do so. Children have not yet developed inhibitions about religious beliefs and activities. In fact, given the right kind of support and incentives, children will always surprise you with how forthright they are in inviting friends to a parish activity geared to their interests.

Let's begin with a few "what ifs."

What if your Sunday school had a special celebration format one Sunday a month, focusing on some religious theme (different every month). Children would attend their regular classes on these Sundays, but their class time would be shortened to allow for a festivity with cake and punch and special music in which the various classes could participate. To be manageable in larger congregations, festive events would need to cluster by departments or specified age groups. Classes might take turns acting out a modern version of some biblical theme or story. (No more than five minutes.) At each event I would return to one or two favorite songs, so the children get to know them well and sing with gusto. Children might accompany the music with drums, noise makers, or rhythm instruments.

Engage the creativity of your Sunday school faculty as you brainstorm ways of making this ten- to fifteen-minute period action oriented and fast moving. Each teacher might ask the children what would make Sunday school a more exciting place for them. If taken as criticism, these "moments of truth" might be painful to bear, but an open teacher will gain helpful insights. Should you begin taking some of the children's suggestions seriously, be prepared for a surprise. If given half a chance, the creativity and ingenuity of the children in our churches will bowl us over. They simply need to know that we are willing to test out some of their ideas.

What if these monthly celebrations included a consistent emphasis on encouraging the children to invite friends to these special times? Once they have come to anticipate the fun, surprise, serendipity, and music of these monthly celebrations, they would be motivated to invite their friends.

What if you awarded prizes to the children in various age groups who had invited more friends than anyone else? Prizes might be religious videos, Biblical Trivial Pursuit, or even a special Bible or hymnal. Some adults might see this as bribing the children to coerce their friends into coming to Sunday school. The key will be continually emphasizing the deeper reasons for inviting friends to attend class. If your Sunday school children have not caught these deeper reasons for inviting their friends, possibly they are not hearing the Gospel on a regular basis.

The prizes are simply a way of letting your children know that you are serious about wanting them to bring their friends with them. The prizes also give you a regular opportunity to remind them to think about which friends they will want to invite.

When there is energy and excitement at church, children rarely keep it to themselves. They begin to talk about it with their friends, and their friends will naturally become curious and be open to an invitation.

What if you really did have a jump in attendance, with some of these children attending regularly? You would face the challenge of engaging their parents in your congregation.

What if your Religious Education Committee took on the task of holding an adult forum track on topics of special interest to parents, such as:

— kids and drugs
— how to talk to your child about sexual issues
— how to nurture honesty in your child
— rituals that build family cohesiveness
— biblical passages that make for excellent parent-child dialogue
— how to teach children to pray
— television, values, and kids

Even if you are not able to engage many parents of new Sunday school children, such a series is bound to engage your regular members in some important issues. It might convince some adult members to invite nonchurched friends, who might bring their children to Sunday school while they attend forum. (Note, if you want to draw a heterogeneous group to your church, be sure to offer more than one adult forum track—one or more classes that would interest nonparents.)

Yes, what if you really did build up some energy in your Sunday school? What ripple effect would it have on your entire congregation? The point is, you need to start somewhere, building excitement in some part of your church life if you want to grow numerically. Consider the payoffs of starting with your Sunday school and children's ministry.

Our research clearly showed that children bring their parents to church, meaning that upon the birth of a first child, parents who have not been affiliated with a congregation often think of returning to church. Out of a concern that their child have the best in religious and moral upbringing, they reconsider their lack of church involvement. This is one reason why growing churches make their nurseries the most attractive rooms in their buildings, and those nurseries are attended by qualified and caring people.

After the nursery comes the Sunday school. These days parents look at church affiliation with a consumer mindset. They shop for the local congregation that offers their child the best quality Sunday school experience.

If nothing else, these suggestions will focus your attention on upgrading the quality of your Sunday school and children's ministry. Given what we have learned from our research on church growth, improvements in this area have more potential payoff than most any other evangelism activity you could devise.

What if Sunday school became such an exciting place to be in your parish that you had more people volunteer to teach classes than you could use?

[end of homework]

Centering

"With your eyes closed, pay attention to your breath. Listen to your body. Relax. Head, neck, and back aligned. Feet on the floor. Breathe deeply. In. Out. Again. Again.

"Go back in time. Imagine yourself as a child. Center on one childhood experience that stands out, maybe it symbolizes the tone of your whole childhood. How old were you? Linger in that scene for a moment. How did that day—and others in your child-hood—affect who you are today?

"Jesus said that unless we become as little children, we cannot enter into the king-dom of God. Meditate on that saying of Jesus'. What is there about childhood that pre-pares a person to enter into the kingdom of God? As an adult, how and when and where are you able to reenter that graced state? When was the last time you felt you were in a childlike state? Place yourself in that scene and linger there for a moment.

"When you are ready, focus again on your breathing. Then slowly open your eyes."

Team Building

Give participants sixty seconds each to talk about thoughts and feelings that came to them as they meditated on Jesus' saying that unless we become as children we cannot enter God's kingdom.

Class Activity

Summarize, review, and discuss the assigned reading. The plan described in the reading will undoubtedly upset the normal routine of a Sunday school. If your church were to increase its Sunday school attendance by fifteen to thirty percent, what would be the ramifications? Allow no more than ten minutes for this discussion.

Have participants work in groups of three or four. Any Sunday school teachers, workers, or Christian Education Committee members present should be spread around, so their experience and information benefits as many groups as possible. You might also have parents of children in specific classes integrated throughout the groups. (If you have two parents of second graders, put them in two separate groups, so their experiences benefit a greater number.) Ask participants to open their workbooks to this page and, using the following scale, work together in small groups to rate the priority your church places on children's ministry. (Option: Have groups walk through the building, assess-ing the classroom space.) Give groups fifteen to twenty minutes for this exercise.

Rating Our Church's Priority on Children's Ministry

A. Money budgeted for children's ministry

	1	2	3	4	5	6	
Low priority						High priority	

B. Quality of classroom space

	1	2	3	4	5	6	
Low priority						High priority	

C. Recruitment of quality persons to teach Sunday school

    1   2   3   4   5   6
  Low priority   High priority

D. Extent to which children are welcomed and engaged in other congregational activities besides Sunday school

    1   2   3   4   5   6
  Low priority   High priority

E. Quality Sunday school curriculum

    1   2   3   4   5   6
  Low priority   High priority

F. Quality of "extra" activities in Sunday school (beyond teaching the lesson)

    1   2   3   4   5   6
  Low priority   High priority

G. Overall rating of our church in relation to children's ministry

    1   2   3   4   5   6
  Low priority   High priority

Back in a large group, have small groups report their overall rating. What factors influenced their decisions? Then through discussion come to a group consensus on an overall rating.

Discuss ways you might support the Sunday school and children's ministry so that it can become a key strength of the parish. How can the Sunday school be a vehicle that supports the church's evangelistic outreach? Your discussions might include answers to these questions: What people first need to get excited about this prospect? What committees need to catch the vision for any proposed changes? Let's say you had an influx of Sunday school children in the next six months, what would you have to do to retain those children? Are teacher training and curriculum and program evaluation prerequisites for retaining children brought in?

On newsprint list your findings in goal language. Prioritize them and then work on strategies for accomplishing objectives.

Save these goals for Session 15.

Homework Assignment

Tell participants to read before the next session the "Class Assignment" that begins on page 65.

Closing

End the session with prayer, mentioning especially the children of the parish and the children's workers.

Notes

Goals for children's ministry:

_____

_____

_____

_____

_____

_____

_____

_____

_____

_____

_____

_____

_____

_____

_____

_____

_____

_____

_____

_____

_____

_____

_____

Notes continued . . .

SESSION NINE

Remaining Open to Inviting Friends to Church

Class Assignment

Before Session 9, participants should read the following article, "Inviting Friends and Family Members to Church."

Inviting Friends and Family Members to Church

Two statistics provide critical information for this session. The first we read in session 8. It bears repeating: What brought you to this church?

   2 percent—an advertisement
   6 percent—an invitation by the pastor
   6 percent—an organized evangelistic outreach program
   86 percent—an invitation by a friend or family member

The second question is this: What brought you to seek a church family?

   50 percent—had just moved into the area
   10 percent—were moving into a marital relationship
   40 percent—were experiencing some sort of crisis or transition

The first set of statistics indicates that a personal invitation is a far more potent force for congregational growth than any other type of organized evangelism effort. Regardless of their insight or devotion, known persons simply have more credibility than strangers.

The second set of statistics needs a little more explanation. In our study we discovered that about half the people seeking out church membership had recently moved geographically. Some churches do a better job than others at reaching out to people who have just moved into their vicinity.

About ten percent of those seeking out a church are wanting a church wedding. In this country people still feel that weddings belong in a church. Some congregations see this as a ministry and reach out to these couples with premarital counseling and other programs geared to young couples.

The remaining forty percent sought a church family because they were going through some sort of transition. The predominant transition named was the birth of a first child. Some congregations have grown significantly simply by focusing in on couples having their first child. One congregation attending an Alban Assimilation of New Members Workshop told of the church's success when a member sent notes of congratulation and the offer of a free gift from the church (if they would call to request it) to the parents listed each week in a "new births" column in the local newspaper. The gift was a Bible. When new parents called, a volunteer from the church delivered the Bible and invited them to a Sunday morning worship service. One out of every five persons receiving a Bible came to visit the congregation at least once. That's an amazing statistic: twenty percent. It indicates how much more receptive people are to an invitation when they have a newborn.

Most of the remainder of the forty percent "in transition" were going through some sort of crisis. They had just lost jobs or relationships or their kids had been arrested for being on drugs or their parents had just died or become seriously ill. Because of their crises, these people realized they were hanging out there all alone without any religious community, or any other community for that matter, that cared about them. Many of these people had grown up in the church and had simply gotten away from it. Their crises motivated them to start looking for an appropriate church family.

Combining these two statistics, we find that people are going to be most receptive to an invitation to attend a church when (1) they are going through some sort of transition (moving, marriage, or personal crisis) and (2) they are invited during that time by someone they know and trust.

In this session, we will focus on the implications of these findings: What do they mean for you as a congregation? What do they mean for you as individuals?

To consider the congregational implications: How can you get the loyal members of your congregation to be more inviting of their friends and family members, especially when these acquaintances are experiencing life transitions?

For the most part our study revealed that members of mainline churches are loath to invite their friends to church. Reasons for this range from a lack of confidence in articulating why one attends church to not wishing to impose faith issues on others. After all, isn't religion a private matter that should never be talked about in public? Yet many do not invite their acquaintances simply because they are not being asked to by their congregations. When I ask workshop participants if their congregations have at least a yearly invite-a-friend Sunday, maybe five or ten percent raise a hand. What a lost opportunity for outreach and growth.

[end of homework]

Centering

"Let's quiet ourselves for a moment and become aware of physical sensations. Close your eyes and focus on one of your physical senses and its immediate 'touch.' Do you feel the chair as it supports your weight? The movement of air as it caresses your hands and face? The moisture in your mouth and any taste that lingers in your mouth? (Point out any obvious, then subtle, sounds in the room.) Do you feel the air in your nostrils or mouth as you breathe? Through these sensations, can you feel—hear, taste—ways in which God is manifest and available to you—right now? As present as your breath, your chair. God is around us at all times; we need only eyes to see and ears to hear. God is always more ready to communicate to us than we are to listen, more ready to bestow Grace upon us than we are to receive it. Remain silent a moment to see if you can perceive, sense, the presence of God here and now. *(Long pause.)*

"With your eyes still closed, reach out and clasp the hands of the people next to you. God is present in your neighbor. Allow yourself to feel God in the warm—or cold—hand. In what other ways do you experience God through relationship and community? *(Pause.)* When you are ready, slowly open your eyes and join the large group. Have participants pair up with one person near them. For three minutes, have the two tell each other what sensations and thoughts occurred to them in the silent centering period."

Team Building

Give participants one minute each to tell the group about the circumstance of their first coming to this parish. Were they invited by a friend or family member? Were they facing a life transition or crisis? Had they just moved to this neighborhood? For fun, and to introduce the class activity, you might want to see how your group sampling matches —or doesn't match—the percentages presented in the "Class Assignment" reading.

Class Activity

To encourage class discussion, post the two sets of research statistics on newsprint. Review and summarize the homework reading, if possible drawing from the participants' own church-seeking experiences.

Becoming an Inviting Congregation

The reading focusedon the congregational implications of the research statistics. Follow up the reading by discussing these questions: What can our congregation do to improve its outreach to people facing life transitions, including a household move? What can our congregation do to challenge its members to invite friends and family to be a part of the parish community? Is an invite-a-friend Sunday feasible? Spend thirty minutes on this discussion.

Whether or not you think an invite-a-friend Sunday really works, it does give the membership an opportunity to think about people they might invite to church with them. It also gives a congregation an opportunity to plan a special welcome Sunday, with extra-special music, a pot luck, children's events, and so forth. For months in advance the pastor can announce the coming of this event and get people thinking about unchurched friends who are going through some sort of life transition; a special service is planned with them in mind.

Personal Invitations

The rest of this session focuses on the personal implications of the research statistics. Ask participants to turn to the "Notes" section at the end of this session (page 70). Ask them to work in silence for three minutes writing down the names of as many people as they can who meet both of these criteria: (1) not currently *active* in a congregation (they may claim to belong to another parish but have not been active for years) and (2) currently going through some sort of transition or crisis.

This exercise should raise some awareness of persons whom participants might invite to church some Sunday. (This exercise might be repeated by a pastor during the announcements portion of a worship service to raise awareness of all members.)

At this point ask participants for reasons why they could not possibly invite one of the people on their list to church. Have the group break into small groups of three or four to talk about their hang-ups with giving personal invitations. Allow ten minutes for discussion, then invite participants back to the large group. Set up a role play or two to act out invitation scenarios. Have one role play be in an office setting. One colleague has just gone through a divorce. In a conversation about the pain of this event, have a co-worker try to offer an invitation to attend church some Sunday morning that does not seem intrusive or invasive. For example, "Jack/Mary, I know you are going through a lot of personal hell right now. Whenever I've had some type of personal crisis, I have usually gotten something out of my membership in my church. One of these Sundays you'd be welcome to attend a worship service with me." Try another role play of two people having lunch together; one is talking about a critically ill parent. See if the other person can gently work in an invitation to worship.

At the beginning of this seminar we talked about participants being able to work through some of their hang-ups about inviting a friend to church. Try to gain a commitment on the part of participants to make at least one attempt at inviting to church one person on their list. Ask them to place a star next to the name they think they might be able to ask. Also point out that the Holy Spirit might show them the perfect, unexpected opportunity.

From here on through the end of the seminar, soon after the opening centering, ask if anyone can share a personal experience of inviting a friend or family member to church. I believe many would invite more freely if they knew a group of people stood behind them, being there to hear their stories.

Draw the session to a close with these remarks: Working through our personal fears and apprehensions is important if a congregation is to become more inviting. It is folly to think that other people are going to invite people to visit the parish when we are not even willing to try it ourselves. Every congregation needs a core group that has had some experience at this to challenge and encourage other members to do the same. Remember the statistic: eighty-six percent of those attending a church for the first time are there because some friend risked asking them to give the church a try.

Homework Assignment

Ask participants to read before the next session the "Class Assignment" on pages 71-74

Closing

The closing prayer could be a petition for faith, skill, and courage at becoming a more inviting person on behalf of God's goodness and mercy.

Notes

Ways our congregation can improve its outreach to people facing transitions:

_____

_____

_____

_____

_____

_____

_____

_____

_____

_____

_____

_____

_____

People not currently active in a congregation who are facing a transition or crisis:

_____

_____

_____

_____

_____

_____

_____

_____

_____

_____

_____

_____

_____

_____

The Power of an Effective Follow-Up

Class Assignment

Before Session 10, participants should read the following article, "Identifying Newcomers and Effective Follow-Up."

Identifying Newcomers and Effective Follow-Up

Let's start a discussion of how to carry out an effective follow-up to parish visitors by stating the obvious: Without a name and address no follow up is possible.

This fact places many mainline churches in a predicament, as they want to be sensitive to persons who want to remain anonymous until they have thoroughly checked out a congregation. The Myers-Briggs Type Indicator points out some important differences between extraverts and introverts. Extraverts usually want to meet and talk with people on their first visits. They use the outer world of people, events, and things to check out a congregation. Many introverts, on the other hand, want to experience a place first, then go home to think about what they saw, heard, and felt before they engage the people there. The worst thing to do on a Sunday morning is to ask visitors to stand up and introduce themselves. You're prompting a worst-case scenario for most introverts, who may have nightmares about standing up and speaking in front of a crowd.

Yet the ground rule for effective new-member development still stands: Before a visitor leaves the building, several attempts should have been made to secure a name and address.

Many congregations use a guest book for this purpose. Unfortunately, most visitors will not sign the guest book unless someone specifically invites them to do so. Other congregations have pew cards that visitors can fill out and place in the offering plate. Once again, few visitors will take the initiative to do this unless they are specifically invited to do so at some point in the worship service. Even then many will conveniently forget to do it.

An increasingly popular practice is called the "ritual of friendship." A notebook especially designed for this purpose is placed at the end of each pew. During the announcement period, everyone in attendance signs in with a name and address—yes even the old timers who have claimed the same pew for twenty-five years. There are clear advantages to this practice, which does take effort to monitor. As the notebook is passed down the row, members can note the names of any visitors sitting in their pew. One hopes that members will introduce themselves to those visitors after the worship service.

This also provides a way for congregations to track the attendance of their members. Congregations that do not take the time and effort to track the attendance patterns of their members and follow through when patterns are broken will have people falling away from the church and staying away permanently. The research of John Savage in his book *The Apathetic and Bored Church Member* (Reynoldsburg, OH: LEAD Consultants, 1976) reveals some frightening statistics. Savage discovered that bored or apathetic members often were once strongly committed, but then some critical incident made them stay away from church for a Sunday or two. Sometimes the critical incident took place in the church; feelings were hurt. Sometimes an incident that had nothing to do with the church; maybe a son or daughter was arrested for being on drugs; maybe the member lost a job and became too embarrassed to attend church the next Sunday. Either way, a member ended up staying away from church for several Sundays. Then another type of hurt or anger crept in: "I thought I was important to some of the people at the church. But no one called to ask if anything was wrong. Must be no one cares whether or not I attend." This can motivate members to stay away even longer. Once they have stayed away from Sunday worship for two to three months, new Sunday morning activities have become habitual. According to Savage, it is more difficult to reactivate your bored or apathetic members than it is to gain new members. This is one strong reason for a congregation being intentional about tracking the worship patterns of its members and having someone monitor those patterns carefully. Once a pattern is broken, the pastor or another key person is notified so an immediate follow through can be made.

The other clear reason for instituting this "ritual of friendship" is to gain a name and address of every visitor to your church on Sunday morning. Visitors are not isolated or threatened in this activity, as everyone in the church is asked to participate.

The worst thing to do is to gain names and addresses of visitors and then do nothing with them. Many congregations immediately mail all visitors a letter, thanking them for their visit and telling them a little about the congregation. A better activity is a follow-up telephone call. This makes for a more personal touch, potentially allowing the callers to find out important information that assists in further follow-up activity with these visitors.

Best of all is a personal home visit the very afternoon of the first Sunday morning church visit. I am not recommending a formal call, where you try to gain access into people's homes and talk for an hour. I am recommending a brief chat in the doorway, probably delivering some token of friendship, such as a freshly baked loaf of bread, a bag of cookies, or a pie. This is by no means a pressure call but a gentle touch, thanking people for visiting the parish and inviting them to ask questions they might have. Should you be invited in, you should usually decline, saying you do not want to impose on people's private time and space. Should your parish have a new-member packet or brochure, you might deliver this.

Knocking on a stranger's door without anything to deliver can be frightening. But delivering a freshly baked bag of cookies and a new-member packet looks easy, especially if you are invited *not* to accept an invitation to enter the home unless you really feel comfortable doing so. Having a freshly baked "something" in the home of the visitor that evening can leave a very favorable impression of your church. Choose the person who makes the best pies, cookies, or bread in the congregation and see if, for the sake of your congregation growing, that person would be willing to have some on hand at all times. (The congregation should offer to reimburse that member for expenses.)

Let's back up a minute to address the question of who should make the visit—and when.

Dramatic statistics indicate that the timing of the visit is crucial. When follow-up visits are made within twenty-four hours of the parish visit, seventy percent return the following Sunday. The response declines from this optimal point, dropping to thirty percent when home visits are made two weeks after the initial parish visit. It seems the parish visitors leave worship service still undecided about any future participation. But a follow-up visit that same afternoon can tip the balance: Yes, this really is a warm, friendly congregation that I'd like to try again.

As for "who"—our research on new-member assimilation revealed that a follow-up visit made by a lay person often makes a deeper impression on the parish visitor than an initial call being made by the pastor. People expect the clergy to make visitors feel welcome. But, they ask, *does anyone else in the congregation care if I return?* Lay visitation teams can make a dramatic impact on parish visitors. The medium is the message: Lay persons in this congregation care enough about their church to make follow-up calls on visitors.

Let's also consider the effect lay visitation teams might have when visitors return to the church the next Sunday. The returning parish visitors will be looking to see the familiar faces of the "callers." And usually the "callers" will be looking for the visitors. Who wouldn't wonder if the visit really did pay off? One hopes the two parties see each other and chat for a minute.

At this point some careful matching of parish visitor with those doing the follow-up visiting becomes important. It is a plain, simple fact that people are unlikely to continue to visit a parish if they do not connect with other people with whom they feel comfortable, with whom they share similar problems, values, lifestyles. As far as possible, members making the follow-up visits should match the age, social standing, income level, and lifestyle of the persons being visited. There will never be a perfect match here, so simply do the best you can.

This match-up will require considerable organization after a Sunday morning service. In a small church, greeters at the door might be able to remember names and characteristics of visitors. In a larger church, this expectation is unrealistic. You might try backing up the ritual of friendship notebooks (which collect names and addresses) with "visitor spotters" who are "planted" in every fourth pew. These would be members who agree to sit in a certain pew every week, noting age and other characteristics of visitors in their pew and the three pews ahead of them. After the service these "spotters" could collect the ritual of friendship notebooks from those four rows and meet briefly to report observations to a coordinator who would assign visitation teams.

Each congregation would need to determine whether to have these calls made by a well-trained cadre of follow-up visitors or to draw on all members of the congregation, who, though untrained, would provide a larger pool from which to match lifestyle interests of particular visitors. With untrained members, it's especially important to give them something, such as a new-member packet and something freshly baked, to "drop off" at the home of the parish visitor. Give some slight coaching and encouragement. Hand the person a three-by-five card with two statements and three questions on it—cues as to what the parish visitor should say when dropping off the bread and brochure. The card could read as follows:

> Thank you for visiting [name of church].
> 1. Do you have any questions about our congregation based on
>   your first visit with us?
> 2. Do you know what you are looking for in a church family?
> 3. Would you like the pastor to make a call on you?
>   We hope you will worship with us again.

Any detailed plan for visitor follow-up requires a committed group of coordinators. Especially if you ask an untrained member to make a follow-up call, someone needs to phone that person to debrief the experience. Thank such members for their efforts and encourage them to try to greet and nurture their particular parish visitors on succeeding Sundays.

Centering

"Let's gather again, unified in silence. If nothing else, this reflection provides a pause between the routine or stress of the day and our study time as a community. In a few minutes we'll challenge our perceptions and behaviors. But right now let's center on personal and spiritual nourishment.

"Close your eyes and focus first on your breathing. Breathe deeply, in, out. Relax that tightened muscle in your neck, your back. What is causing that knot? Acknowledge the concern on your mind and set it aside for a season. How do you view yourself as you sit here? Can you see yourself as God does—with unconditional love—loving you just as you are? Where two or three are gathered together in the name of God, there we find Christ in our midst."

After a period of silence, someone may offer a prayer invoking the presence of the Spirit to be evident in your midst as you struggle with issues of reaching out to others with the nontangible offering of spiritual truth.

Team Building

Give participants sixty seconds each to tell the group about the one person who most reached out to them when they started attending this congregation. Who was this person and in what ways did he or she reach out?

Debriefing

Ask if any participants have invited a friend to church. Invite any who have to relate the experience, good or bad.

Class Activity

Summarize and review the homework assignment as it relates to your own parish.

Identifying Newcomers

First, look at how well your parish identifies newcomers, obtaining names and addresses. What is your current system? As things are now, how and where do visitors "fall through the cracks"? How might these cracks be closed up? Does the current system need slight reinforcement or major overhaul? Spend no more than ten minutes writing goals for how to better identify newcomers.

Tracking Members

You might briefly address whether the "ritual of friendship" notebooks would suit your needs in terms of tracking members who quit attending for a while. Though this is an important item, it can potentially sidetrack the group from the issue of visitor follow up. Spend no more than ten minutes on this issue. If the group agrees that this is a real problem that hasn't been addressed in previous sessions, make note of this and continue your discussion of solutions in Session 15.

Visitor Follow-Up

Turn to the topic of visitor follow-up. What does your parish currently do in this regard? Letters? Telephone calls? Visits? By whom? When? Review the statistics that indicate calls are most effective the day of the first visit. Is this feasible for your congregation? What are the obstacles? Benefits?

If home visits are feasible, what are the benefits of having a small group of well-trained calling teams? How does this weigh against asking any member of the church to make a call on a "matched" visitor? Work on goals and strategies for contacting visitors after their first visit. What organizational systems would you need?

What printed materials do you now have that would make up a new-member packet? What additional or revised materials would be more effective? I would not recommend overloading this packet with too many items. No need to include the annual report of the parish, for example, which no doubt gives more detail than any first-time visitor cares to see. What other items would a visitor take to and leave with a newcomer? What could you use for immediate visits? What would work best in the long run?

Identify several goals that would improve your newcomer follow-up.

Bring the idea of making follow-up calls down to a personal level. This will be easier than inviting a friend or family member to church. Here you have someone already motivated to look for a church family and a suitable worship community. Here you're simply extending a personal welcome for your congregation.

What items are persons going to deliver to the visitors' homes? What parish literature do you have in print that you could place in the hands of parish visitors?

Role Plays

For practice, role play several home visits. Ask for a volunteer to choose a visitor identity (i.e., a single, older female; a single, older male; a young couple with two children.) A second person should play-act a Sunday afternoon visit to the home of the first. Then have another two people act out a second scenario. Take time to debrief each role play, having participants add comments and suggestions.

Try to gain a commitment from everyone to make such a follow-up call at some point in the next few weeks. Through the church office and whatever system you currently have in place, provide each participant (if possible) with the name and address of someone who has visited the church in the last two weeks (or month).

Give instructions that if no one answers the door, callers should leave the literature and bread and telephone later to introduce themselves and express the welcome.

Homework Assignment

Ask participants to read before the next session the "Class Assignment" on pages 79-81.

Closing

Ask someone to offer a prayer asking for insight and courage as people move out to welcome parish newcomers.

Notes

Goals for identifying visitors and contacting them after their visit to the church:

_____

_____

_____

_____

_____

_____

_____

_____

_____

_____

_____

_____

_____

_____

_____

_____

_____

_____

_____

_____

_____

_____

_____

_____

_____

_____

_____

_____

Notes continued . . .

Requirements of Membership

Class Assignment

Before Session 11 participants should read the following article, "Requirements of Membership."

Requirements of Membership

Session 11 will focus on issues of church membership. What does membership in your congregation mean to you?

Our research on the incorporation of new members into congregations revealed that mainline Protestant churches are timid when it comes to inviting people into membership. Most congregations we studied asked very little of those who had decided to join the church. Only two out of the twenty-two congregations we studied asked potential members to take on a spiritual discipline as part of becoming a member of the parish. No congregation was explicit about what it expected of persons joining in terms of worship attendance and participation in other parish activities. Most intimated that persons joining would be asked to help out financially, yet no congregation laid out guidelines as to how much members were striving to give (i.e., a tithe). We concluded that churches are usually so eager to have people join that they in effect say, "We don't expect a whole lot from you; just come and be a part of us."

As we made this observation in the churches we studied, we also realized that the fastest growing denominations in the U.S. are not at all timid about laying out requirements for membership. If you join the Mormon Church, for example, it is made quite clear that you will be required to tithe your income (give ten percent to the church), attend worship every Sunday, become active in a family cluster group, and so forth. In these high-requirement denominations, membership tends to take on a deeper meaning. The Church of the Saviour in Washington, D.C., has put much thought into the issue of membership. This is detailed in the book *Call to Commitment* by Elizabeth O'Connor. As a prerequisite to membership in that parish, one needs to take on a two-year study commitment. That congregation has always had more persons active than were actual members. People are welcome to affiliate with the parish, and when they are ready to take on the commitments of membership, they are invited to take that further step.

Assuming the absence of clear definitions of membership in your parish, let's explore what could be some clear messages you could give persons joining the church. What is expected of members of the parish? It will be quite disillusioning to newcomers if they are asked to adhere to certain standards of membership and later discover no one else in the congregation is living up to those standards.

A place to begin is with some deeper requirements related to attendance at a series of newcomer classes as a prerequisite for joining. I recommend that you press for a minimum of six two-hour sessions with all who express a desire to join your parish, even those who have been lifelong members of your denomination. Look at these classes from a new angle. The main purpose should not be to indoctrinate persons into denominational belief systems. Rather, consider the following reasons for requiring instruction of potential joiners:

1. **Sharing of religious journeys.** I recommend that at least fifty percent of the time in these new-member classes be spent in having participants listen to each other's life experiences. Why not use this time to become acquainted with the spiritual pilgrimage of those persons desiring to join your parish? You might have each newcomer draw his or her spiritual and emotional lifeline on a sheet of paper, then present this to the class. This information will assist you in assimilating newcomers into the ongoing life of your parish. It also assists you in planning for the new members' continuous growth in grace and faith.

2. **Bonding with other newcomers.** Your newcomers need to develop some indepth relationships with others in the parish. If this type of bonding does not occur, they are less likely to remain active. Why not encourage bonding with the old timers of the parish? You will want to provide opportunities for such interaction (as in matching visitation teams with newcomers). But realistically your old timers probably have their lives filled with as many relationships in the parish as they can manage. When your old timers come to church on Sunday, they want to connect with old friends. They are already part of a clique, and you want new cliques to be forming all the time. To a certain degree, cliques are good for a parish. You want everyone to feel as if he or she has a special relationship with a handful of other members. By requiring at least six two-hour sessions in which newcomers meet together, you are allowing people to be drawn in to the lives of a small group of parishioners. As they talk about their spiritual journeys, they will most likely become invested in one another's lives. When they attend services and activities, they will have a special kinship with at least this handful of other members of the parish. For the above to be accomplished, the class needs to be a certain size—no fewer than four. But it's hard to build community when a class becomes larger than twelve.

3. **Quality time with your pastor.** Clergy are busy people. Without some structured time when newcomers have your pastor to themselves for a series of sessions, an adequate bonding between the pastor and newcomers may not take place.

4. Sharing the history, symbols, and norms of the parish plus your expectations for members. Persons wishing to join your parish may be lifelong members of your denomination, very familiar with the doctrine, liturgy, and practice of your judicatory. But your congregation has been on a spiritual pilgrimage of its own. The norms of your parish grow out of your congregation's history. If newcomers are to grasp the sense of this parish, they will need to know more about its inner life. Here you begin to talk about what membership means to long-term members and what the congregation expects of its members. (More on this later.)

5. Religious beliefs of your denomination. Participation in new-member classes should also be a faith-deepening experience. This is a prime time to present basic Christian beliefs and any doctrinal position held by your denomination. In this regard, a textbook may be helpful. Yet class participation should be central to all sessions, allowing participants to get to know one another and the pastor and staff to get to know the newcomers and their belief systems.

To cover these objectives, you may need even more than six two-hour classes. Done well, these classes will be a meaningful experience for your joiners, heightening the significance of their church membership.

Aside from a newcomers' class, what requirements might you present as people join the church? If your congregation does not currently have strict requirements for membership, it is unlikely that you will be able to force these on the parish now. Yet effort in this area can contribute to a congregation's renewal. It's a way of inviting members into a deeper commitment to their church.

I recommend starting with members of this workshop. What would be a standard for membership that you all could agree on? I would discourage you from becoming legalistic about this. (There is a demonic side to legalism that I don't wish on anyone.) Yet what reasonable standard can you all subscribe to? This standard could include attendance at Sunday worship, financial contributions, personal spiritual disciplines, participation in other parish activities, and seeing one's daily vocation as a ministry.

Centering

"Close your eyes and quiet your spirits. Listen to your breath. What do you hear? Feel?

"Every emotional experience has its corresponding breathing pattern. When we are stressed, our breath grows rapid and shallow. When we we are shocked, we stop breathing. When we are deeply relaxed, we breathe easy, long, and deep. As you listen to your breath, what does it tell you about your current state of mind?

"Consciously allow your breaths to grow longer and deeper. That pattern relaxes the body. Breathe out the tension. Let go.

"Total relaxation is a very appropriate response to God's free gift of Grace. Since there is nothing we can do to earn God's Grace, we might as well relax into it. Imagine yourself in the palm of God's hand. God is looking down upon you with deep compassion. Nestle into your chair as if it were the palm of God's compassionate hand.

"Stay with this image and this state of relaxation for a few minutes. Though many things may not be going as well as you wish, place your cares within the enfolding peace of God. If disturbing thoughts try to draw you away from this image, let them float on by like a cloud, then return to the warmth of being in the palm of God's hand. You might silently repeat the words, 'Grace and Peace, Grace and Peace.'"

Following the silent portion of this centering time, have someone close with a prayer, invoking God's continued presence during the session.

Team Building

Have participants take sixty seconds and tell the group the high point and the low point of their day. If you're meeting in the morning, have them share the high and low point of the week.

Debriefing

Ask if any participants have invited a friend to Sunday worship or visited a parish visitor. Invite any who have to relate briefly the experience, good or bad. Where appropriate, encourage group applause and support. If most class participants have experiences to share, you might divide into small groups for this debriefing. Allow no more than fifteen minutes for this activity. These debriefings can be strong learning experiences. They can also move your congregation into being a more inviting place to visit.

Class Activity

Summarize and review the homework reading. Encourage an open discussion on the subject of requirements for membership.

Give participants five minutes to work alone and write out some potential goals or expectations for membership in this parish. They should list only expectations to which they would be willing to subscribe. Have them write in the "Notes" section at the end of this workbook session.

Ask participants to report on their lists. On newsprint record a comprehensive list and then work with the group to arrive at a consensus. Which membership goals are realistic?

If the group reaches a consensus (it might not), develop a strategy for presenting these membership goals to your congregation's chief decision-making body for its consideration. I don't suggest that you ask that body to approve these as standards for the congregation. Ask instead if these expectations for membership are ones to which the majority of them could subscribe.

Invite them to revise your list so that all of that group and this workshop group could agree on goals for membership. Ask a participant to read aloud the following "Class Reading."

Class Reading

Between this workshop group and your chief decision-making body, you no doubt have enough of a critical mass to begin exploring this with the remainder of the congregation. Even though it would be difficult to get an entire congregation to agree on such goals or expectations for membership (and I don't recommend that you try), you can at least say that the core leadership of the parish is striving to live up to these standards. With that base of support, you can go before your newcomers who wish to join and say, "In this congregation we are attempting to reach these goals for membership." Believe me, such a statement would be considerably more concrete than that given by most mainline parishes on this continent.

An example: We, the members of this parish, strive to be in worship at least three Sundays out of four. We strive to give five percent of our income to charity and our church. We support one another in our attempts to see our daily vocation as the most central part of our ministry. We attempt to exercise daily prayer and to say a grace-prayer at at least one meal a day.

If, as pastor of a congregation, I felt the core leadership of the parish made a conscious attempt to live up to these membership goals, I would have no qualms about relating these membership goals to anyone wishing to become a member of the parish. Over time the level of commitment in the parish would rise considerably because of the intention of key leaders and the challenge placed before everyone who wished to join. Belonging to this parish would no doubt take on a deeper meaning for all who had decided to live up to the challenge.

As a result of the above, this workshop group and/or the chief decision-making body could discuss with the pastor what membership goals he or she would be willing to present in new-member classes.

Homework Assignment

Announce the homework for Session 12, the "Class Assignment" reading on pages 85-87.

Closing

The closing prayer for this session could sum up the class's struggles with issues of commitment and focus on the graciousness of God, who bestows gifts on us daily regardless of our commitment.

Notes

Personal list on what could/should be expected of church members:

_____

_____

_____

_____

_____

_____

_____

_____

_____

_____

_____

_____

Group consensus of expectations of church members:

_____

_____

_____

_____

_____

_____

_____

_____

_____

_____

_____

_____

_____

_____

Going Deeper—Volunteer Management

Class Assignment

Before Session 12, participants should read the following article, "Going Deeper."

Going Deeper

In the research questionnaire used to debrief newcomers on their experience of joining a congregation, we asked what congregations did to invite new members into more active participation. Alas, we discovered that most congregations abandoned people once they had joined, as if the parish then had no further concerns about the newcomers. Once someone had joined it was either sink or swim in terms of becoming part of the congregation or drifting away.

Congregations gain little when people join the parish only to become inactive. From one point of view, this is downright irresponsible of the church. By joining, people are supposedly being brought into the care of the congregation, not being abandoned to their own devices.

Growing congregations that care for their newcomers continue to monitor their activities for at least two years after they have joined. They continue being involved with new members in two major areas: (1) nurturing their spiritual growth and (2) helping them find meaningful volunteer roles to express their faith.

First, let's briefly look at how a church might nurture spiritual growth. In Session 11 I encouraged you to institute at least six two-hour sessions as a prerequisite to people joining the parish. In such an inquirers' class, you may discover that you are welcoming persons at opposite ends of a continuum in terms of instruction in the faith. On the one hand you may have a brand new Christian—a real babe in the faith. This person has had no previous experience in any church. The Bible is a complete mystery. For this person to grow spiritually, the parish is going to have to provide teaching in fundamental Christianity. Without this, this person will remain biblically illiterate and ignorant about basic Christian practice, such as prayer, liturgy, and charity.

On the other hand you may have in the same class someone who has been a church officer, who has been raised in a church of your denomination, and who needs more challenging opportunities to develop spiritually.

This clearly provides a challenge to any parish Christian Education Committee, which should be asking, "Are we providing the right kind of growth opportunities for the people joining our parish?" To do this well, the committee needs to continually dialogue with the pastor and others working with these newcomers to ascertain their level of spiritual maturity. What gaps exist in their spiritual development? If that committee responds to the spiritual needs of newcomers, it might discover that many more in the congregation will want to drink from the same cup.

Let's now turn to how a parish helps its members find meaningful volunteer roles. In our research on people joining congregations, we discovered two parishes, one Lutheran and one Episcopal, that had employed a coordinator of volunteers. Growing congregations, both knew they needed to do a better job at providing meaningful volunteer roles not only for their newcomers but for everyone in the congregation.

It is sad to say that most congregations abuse their volunteers. Prior to our study on new-member assimilation, The Alban Institute was able to complete a study on Lay Leader Burnout. (*How To Prevent Lay Leader Burnout,* 1984) What is the basic anatomy of burnout among key lay leaders? Some leaders are challenged to take on major roles without being informed of the complexity of the roles; to carry out their responsibilities, they depended on the work of other volunteers. As some of these other volunteers did not follow through on their commitments and tasks, these key volunteers grew disillusioned about fellow members. (This type of disillusionment does not usually occur with your average volunteer who teaches a class or sings in the choir.) In time these key volunteers lost their ability to worship on Sunday morning. We saw three reasons: First, on Sunday mornings they were preoccupied, trying to touch base with many others on business matters. Second, when they finally got to sit down in the pew, they would look around at pious members who never accomplished what they said they would. Last, these key volunteers began to lose respect for their clergy. Because of their central role, they saw clergy at their worst; they saw the human side of clergy often hidden from a larger group. One other factor came into play: Once these key volunteers had completed their tenure, they were cast aside for others who assumed the mantle. They often ended up as inactive members, completely disillusioned about their congregation and the whole religious enterprise.

A staff coordinator of volunteers can see that this type of burnout does not occur. This is the person to whom one can turn when a particular volunteer role is beginning to feel bad. The coordinator of volunteers tries to spread out the service roles in the parish so that more than a handful of people are carrying the major burden of parish work.

We need to change the way we think about volunteerism. If we think that someone who volunteers to take on a parish role is doing us a favor, we have got it all backwards. The parish is doing volunteers a favor by offering roles that bring meaning to life, by providing important learnings and opportunities to deepen personal relationships. People don't burn out when they are learning or contributing their gifts to causes that are important to them or working with people they care to be with.

We also need to relinquish thinking that tells us that we cannot demand excellence of volunteers. The opposite is usually the case. The more we demand of volunteers, the more committed they become to their roles. At least they know that someone cares about what they do in their volunteer task. They also know they are going to learn a whole lot more when excellence is demanded of them. Just because we do not pay people money to complete their tasks does not mean that we have little to offer them as reward for their efforts.

Studies on motivation have shown that money ranks fourth or fifth in terms of what motivates people to work hard at tasks assigned to them. The following motivations rank right up there with money:

- being able to learn and grow in a role
- feeling that talents are being well used
- contributing to important causes
- being able to work with people who care about me and about whom I care
- having increased responsibility

A congregation that works hard to provide every parish volunteer with one or two of the above motivators honors its volunteers and practices good stewardship of the parish's volunteer energies. Again, a coordinator of volunteers can oversee this motivational factor.

In regard to newcomers, the coordinator of volunteers usually contracts for an hour-long interview with everyone joining the parish to help determine where motivated skills can be best used in the parish. A coordinator often acts as a midwife to see that committee chairs follow through on inviting participation by persons who have shown an interest in the work of those committees.

Finally, coordinators of volunteers periodically offer learning events at which parish members can identify their motivated gifts at this particular juncture in life. Every person is continually changing and growing. What challenged us two years ago may no longer motivate us to give our best. A six-week course or an all-day Saturday workshop or a parish retreat focusing on gifts identification may help all members discern what God seems to be calling them to do next. (The Alban Institute has published the outline of a course titled *What Do I Have to Offer?* which can be a resource for this type of activity.)

Congregations relying on time-and-talent sheets assume that people know what their motivated gifts are. Many don't. Secular career centers make megabucks helping people discover their talents and gifts. The same needs are present in church volunteers. Many are out of touch with their growing edge. Others are worn down by having stayed in roles out of duty and obligation. Not happy campers, they are spewing negative energy on other volunteers. They need to be replaced by persons who would enjoy the roles but have not been given the opportunities.

Centering

"Close your eyes and focus attention on your heart. Feel its rhythm in your chest. Listen. The heart is not only an important physical organ, it is also a center of feeling. We say, "It broke my heart," to describe a sensation we feel in our heart space. Our heart is a place of deeper knowing. We differentiate head knowledge from heart knowledge.

"Breathe deeply, in and out. Draw that air right into your heart space. As the oxygen surrounds your heart, what emotions does it fit? Is your heart heavy with sorrow? With worry? Is it light with joy? Dwell a minute on your heart concerns.

"Package the concerns that seem to weigh on your heart and send them to God. In prayer, turn your concerns over to God, who is more than willing to take over those burdens for a while so you can enjoy the gift of being totally present with our community, which manifests God's care."

Following an appropriate amount of silence, have someone read aloud Psalm 42, a prayer of longing for God from the heart.

Team Building

Give participants sixty seconds each to talk about an event in the past twelve months that "broke their heart." Other group members should simply listen. No one should attempt to fix anything for someone else. It is gift enough to be present with understanding when someone shares pain. At the conclusion, have someone say a brief prayer that offers all this pain up to God for God's healing action.

Debriefing

Again ask if participants have called on visitors or invited friends to church. Have them relate experiences. If possible, have a few new names and addresses of visitors to give to participants, allowing for timely follow-up.

Class Activity

Review and discuss the homework assignment on a theoretical basis.

Spiritual Nourishment

For no more than fifteen minutes, discuss strengths and weaknesses of your adult Christian education program. Are available classes and groups meeting the needs of all new members? Put any findings in goal language.

Volunteer Management

The following questionnaire is designed to raise awareness of a congregation's current approach to volunteers. This questionnaire will turn the group's attention to the needs of your local parish. Have everyone work alone and complete the survey in silence.

Volunteer Management Survey

The following rating scale has been devised to highlight seventeen key elements in the care and support of volunteers in your congregation. Few if any congregations will score high on every item. Your personal assessment using this scale may assist your congregation in becoming more effective at recruiting, training, and supporting volunteers.

Rate the extent to which your congregation fulfills the following strategies:

A. Provides job descriptions for all volunteer roles in the parish.

      1   2   3   4   5   6

Never   Always

B. Conducts annual discernment of gifts or gifts identification seminar.

      1   2   3   4   5   6

No or low-level program   High-quality program

C. Collects and uses time-and-talent sheets.

      1   2   3   4   5   6

Never   Always

D. Provides, at minimum, an hour-long interview for all newcomers, hearing their histories and helping them discern where they can tie in to church activities.

      1   2   3   4   5   6

Never   Always

E. Asks lay leaders to take only one major role and monitors carefully for burnout.

      1   2   3   4   5   6

Never   Always

F. Evaluates volunteer roles on an annual basis and provides feedback on how roles are being carried out.

      1   2   3   4   5   6

Never   Always

G. Designates someone or some group to oversee the congregational use of volunteers.

      1   2   3   4   5   6

Poor implementation   Well organized

H. Provides sabbatical breaks for teachers and other lay leaders who are especially gifted at specific volunteer roles.

      1   2   3   4   5   6

Never   Regularly

I. Assumes that all members have a sense of being called by God to a certain ministry but may need some help in discerning this call and acting upon it.

      1   2   3   4   5   6

Never   Always

J. Provides long-term strategies for giving capable and motivated persons the opportuni ties to move into leadership positions.

      1   2   3   4   5   6

No strategies   Strong emphasis

K. Continually finds creative ways to say "thank you" to parish volunteers.

      1   2   3   4   5   6

Never   Always

L. Clearly connects the work of volunteers to the ministry of the church.

      1   2   3   4   5   6

Never   Lots of effort

M. Offers training and learning opportunities annually.

      1   2   3   4   5   6

No program   Many opportunities

N. Keeps volunteers informed about developments in the congregation, especially if they affect volunteer roles.

      1   2   3   4   5   6

Poor communications   Strong communications

O. Establishes definite terms of service for all volunteers.

      1   2   3   4   5   6

Never   Always

P. Gives volunteers "exit interviews" after having completed a particularly difficult leader ship assignment.

      1   2   3   4   5   6

Never   Always

Q. Concludes all parish meetings with a brief evaluation of both process and quality of decisions made, so that meetings can be improved.

      1   2   3   4   5   6

Never   Always

Scoring: Add up the numerical rating you gave each question.

Scores of 32 or less   Need for much improvement in use of volunteers

Scores of 33 to 48   Growing competence in use of volunteers

Scores of 49 to 64   Achievement is the reward of much hard work in your management of volunteers

Once everyone has completed the survey, gather as a group and discuss each question individually, arriving at a consensus on that question. This consensus should be more than a cursory averaging out of the numerical responses. Encourage participants to discuss why they gave a certain rating on each question. Try to complete discussion in forty minutes.

Based on the group profile of the parish emerging from this questionnaire, brainstorm some possible goals your parish might adopt to raise its quality of volunteer management. Among other issues, discuss the feasibility or desirability of a staff coordinator of volunteers.

Prioritize your list and choose no more than three or four important goals for the parish to concentrate on over the next twelve months. Once again, you can quickly prioritize by giving everyone in the class three votes, then seeing which goals receive the highest number of votes. Encourage participants to write goals in the "Notes" section at the end of this session. Save these goals for Session 15.

If time allows, be more specific as to strategies for accomplishing your goals.

Homework Assignment

Point out the homework assignment for participants—a reading that starts on page 95.

Closing

The closing prayer can focus on our serving God with our time and talents.

Notes

Goals for our adult Christian education program:

_____

_____

_____

_____

_____

_____

_____

_____

_____

_____

_____

_____

_____

_____

_____

_____

_____

_____

_____

_____

_____

_____

_____

_____

_____

Notes continued . . .

SESSION THIRTEEN

Six Stages for Every Newcomer

Class Assignment

Before class participants should read the following article and fill out the New-Member Assimilation Rating Scale.

The Six Stages of New-Member Development

As we interviewed newcomers to the congregations involved in our research study, we identified a pattern. When things went well for newcomers, they usually passed through six separate stages of development. At each stage there was a chance that the newcomer might not move forward to the next step. That meant that each transition point was a potential crisis point. We saw that some congregations worked hard to assist their new-comers through some of these stages but not through others. In the end we grasped hold of the idea that congregations could learn how to ply quality resources at all six stages of new-member development.

From the newcomer's point of view, we have labeled the six stages as:

1. searching
2. testing
3. returning/affiliating
4. joining
5. going deeper
6. being sent

In our previous twelve sessions, we have dealt with these six stages of development in a variety of ways. In this session we will cover a brief explanation of each stage and then complete a New-Member Assimilation Rating Scale, based on these six stages.

The survey gives you an opportunity to assess how well you think your congregation is helping your newcomers through each of these stages of development.

1. Searching. A crisis or transition usually propels an individual to go out and search for a church family. Fifty percent of those in our study had just geographically relocated and were looking for a suitable church in their new community. For others the transition was the birth of a child, the loss of a job, a marital separation, etc. A congregation aware of this motivation for a search can prepare itself to be more hospitable to people going through a transition.

2. Testing. This refers to the first visit newcomers make to a church. Unless some important things happen on this first visit, they will not return. We often underestimate how threatening it can be to walk into a strange church. Anyone willing to put him- or herself through this angst has to be motivated—looking for something basic that has been missing from life. Is a visitor going to find this in your congregation?

3. Returning/Affiliating. Your congregation has passed the initial first step. Yet the newcomers are still in the negotiating stage. They will not likely return if they don't soon find a small group of people with whom they are compatible and who desire to see them again and again. They are not likely to continue to attend if the doctrines and beliefs of the church are out of sync with their own theological stand. They will also need to like the pastor and feel that the pastor is an "okay" religious authority. Last, the parish hymns and rituals will need to connect with them in some basic way, maybe striking some chord of familiarity with childhood experiences of church.

4. Joining. The decision to join the congregation and commit to the new-member classes is an important milestone. Yet things can go wrong or falter at this stage as well. Since those joining need to feel that the rest of the congregation is pleased with their decision to join, some sort of celebration of the occasion is in order; in addition to a liturgical receiving into membership during Sunday worship, we also recommend a social welcoming event, i.e., a newcomer's dinner or a special coffee hour. As we discussed in Session 11, some important messages about membership are appropriate at this stage.

5. Going deeper. Unfortunately most congregations stop making any effort to continue working with newcomers after stage 4. Yet, as we discussed in Session 12, newcomers often need further help in going deeper spiritually and finding their place through a meaningful volunteer role. Newcomers who do not successfully move through this stage often become inactive and drift to the periphery of the congregation.

6. Being sent. Growing churches try to capitalize on the energy newcomers bring to the parish. The plain fact is, your newcomers are more likely to invite their friends and family members to church than your old timers. New converts are usually the most enthusiastic about the faith, and, having come through the new-member classes, they might know more about your church and your denomination than many of your old timers. What's more, they still have not built up a load of acquaintances in the parish and so are open to being bonded to other newcomers. A great way to involve them in the parish is by asking them to join a lay visitation team that does follow-up calls on parish visitors. This way you have newcomers bonding with other newcomers as you continually form new cliques in the parish.

With this brief explanation of each of the six stages, complete the following New-Member Assimilation Rating Scale. Complete this on your own and be ready to discuss your ratings at the Workshop Session.

New-Member Assimilation Rating Scale

The following rating scale has been designed to help your congregation effectively incorporate new members. Working alone, rate your congregation.

I. Searching

A. The message of faith, hope, and love is proclaimed on a regular basis at our church by both clergy and lay people.

1	2	3	4	5	6
Untrue		Partly true			True

B. The Good News is lived out in the norms of this parish.

1	2	3	4	5	6
Untrue		Partly true			True

C. I am pleased with the variety of ways our congregation attracts newcomers to the parish.

1	2	3	4	5	6
Untrue		Partly true			True

D. I am pleased with the positive image our congregation has in its immediate community because of the various ways we serve the community.

1	2	3	4	5	6
Untrue		Partly true			True

E. Our members regularly invite their nonchurched friends and family members to attend this church with them.

1	2	3	4	5	6
Untrue		Partly true			True

F. Add two points to your score if you have any of the following items by which you may attract newcomers:

____ bells, carillons
____ community newsletter
____ weekly newspaper, radio/TV ads
____ attractive, inviting buildings
____ 24-hour telephone messages for those who call after hours
____ attractive signs on the church exterior communicating times of services
____ day care center, parochial school
____ ad in yellow pages
____ other

G. Add two points for every nonparish community group that uses your facilities on a regular basis.

H. Add two points for every social ministry program that reaches out to people in need in the community:

___ Meals on Wheels   ___ clothing bank
___ soup kitchen   ___ other
___ food pantry

II. Testing

A. Our congregation easily recognizes visitors and has people who go out of their way to make them feel wanted and welcomed.

1	2	3	4	5	6
Untrue		Partly true			True

B. A visitor rarely leaves our congregation without someone getting a name and address for follow-up purposes.

1	2	3	4	5	6
Untrue		Partly true			True

C. Our congregation has a coffee hour following services at which time visitors are approached warmly by parish members.

1	2	3	4	5	6
Untrue		Partly true			True

D. When it is obvious that visitors are lost in our congregation's liturgy, we have persons in the congregation ready to assist them.

1	2	3	4	5	6
Untrue		Partly true			True

E. A card or letter telling people we were glad they visited follows within the week.

1	2	3	4	5	6
Untrue		Partly true			True

F. Simple, clear, printed guides are available for people unfamiliar with the Sunday liturgy.

1	2	3	4	5	6
Untrue		Partly true			True

G. Pew cards are available for visitors to request a visit from the pastor, an information packet, or to be put on the mailing list.

1	2	3	4	5	6
Untrue		Partly true			True

H. All members wear name tags and visitors are given generic "visitor" tags.

1	2	3	4	5	6
Untrue		Partly true			True

III. Returning/Affiliating

Give your congregation the prescribed number of points if you have any of the following:

___ (10) Lay visitation teams that call on visitors in the week following their visit to your church.
___ (6) Lay visitation teams that call on visitors within a month.
___ (10) A staff member who considers calling on parish visitors a priority.
___ (6) A printed brochure/folder that describes the nature of the parish staff.
___ (4) A letter of welcome that is mailed to all parish visitors within a week.
___ (6) A clean, attractive nursery attended by friendly, competent people.
___ (10) A quality Sunday school program
___ (6) An active youth or young adult program.
___ (10) A coordinator of lay volunteers who interviews newcomers when they begin to attend regularly to determine a potential place for them.
___ (10) A variety of small groups (study, service, or decision-making groups) open to newcomers.
___ (10) Short orientation seminars periodically held for visitors.
___ (6) A narrated liturgy periodically held to introduce newcomers and old timers to the history and meaning of the liturgy.

IV. Joining

A. Our congregation requires all potential new members to attend four or more new-member classes.

1	2	3	4	5	6
Untrue		Partly true			True

B. Our congregation makes clear to new members what is expected of them, (i.e., contributions, attendance, etc.)

1	2	3	4	5	6
Untrue		Partly true			True

C. Our congregation invites joiners to observe certain personal spiritual disciplines on their own.

```
        1     2     3     4     5     6
    Untrue           Partly true        True
```

D. Our congregation publicly receives all joiners at a service of worship through a special liturgical event.

```
        1     2     3     4     5     6
    Untrue           Partly true        True
```

E. To celebrate new members joining at a service, our congregation puts on a social event in honor of the joiners, i.e., parish dinner, luncheon with the pastor, etc.

```
        1     2     3     4     5     6
    Untrue           Partly true        True
```

V. Going Deeper

A. Once or twice a year the parish sponsors a "gifts identification" event to assist new members to become more clear about where they feel called in areas of study or service.

```
    1   2   3   4   5   6   7   8   9   10
 Untrue          Partly true        True
```

B. Our parish has persons who regularly monitor the involvement of lay volunteers to ensure prevention of burnout.

```
    1   2   3   4   5   6   7   8   9   10
 Untrue          Partly true        True
```

C. Our parish consistently supports the idea that lay ministry is what Christians do in the world and community, and parish activities support this ministry.

```
    1   2   3   4   5   6   7   8   9   10
 Untrue          Partly true        True
```

D. Our parish has a written job description for every volunteer role in the parish with clear time demands for each role.

```
    1   2   3   4   5   6   7   8   9   10
 Untrue          Partly true        True
```

E. Joiners are interviewed regarding their motivated skills and their growing edge to determine where they might like to contribute their time and talents.

```
    1   2   3   4   5   6   7   8   9   10
 Untrue          Partly true        True
```

VI. Being Sent

A. Our parish consistently invites newcomers to work on new-member-outreach ministries.

1	4	7	10	13	16
Untrue		Partly true			True

B. Our parish consistently challenges parish members to invite and accompany their friends to church.

1	4	7	10	13	16
Untrue		Partly true			True

C. In informal ways the parish supports and praises those who work at inviting and bringing visitors to church.

1	4	7	10	13	16
Untrue		Partly true			True

D. Our parish consistently offers adult seminars geared to helping people be more comfortable talking about matters of personal faith.

1	4	7	10	13	16
Untrue		Partly true			True

Scoring: Add up the numerical ratings for all questions in six parts of this questionnaire.

Good Score for	Corporate Church (350 active plus)	280 or higher
	Program Church (150-350 active)	240 or higher
	Pastoral Church (50-150 active)	220 or higher
Fair Score for	Corporate Church	240 to 280
	Program Church	210 to 240
	Pastoral Church	190 to 220
Poor Score for	Corporate Church	200 or less
	Program Church	180 or less
	Pastoral Church	160 or less

Page five of the NEW MEMBER ASSIMILATION RATING SCALE from *Making Your Church More Inviting*.
Copyright The Alban Institute 1992.

Centering

"We're going to start this session in a few moments of contemplative prayer. The early church practiced two basic forms of prayer: *kataphatic* prayer (Roman School) and *apophatic* prayer (Alexandrian School). In Western Christianity we are generally taught the *kataphatic* form of prayer, which is active and filled with words, images, and concepts: Dear God, thank you for the sunshine this morning, and be with Aunt Doris who is suffering from cancer.

"The *apophatic* form is more the prayer of the mystics who felt you could not contain God in words or images. To experience God they moved to silence rather than to sending words toward God.

"The *apophatic* form of prayer quieted the mind and 'waited' upon the Lord. The person praying in this form desires to hear God in the still, small voice within. We want to ready the ground so God can plant a seed.

"To quiet the mind for this type of prayer, the mystics repeated certain sacred words or phrases to keep their minds from wandering, to keep them in quiet awareness of the wonder of the present. One of the earliest phrases used for this quieting is the Jesus Prayer, sometimes called the prayer of the heart: 'Lord, have mercy.' The Greek form of this prayer is 'Kyrie eleison.' The long form of the prayer is 'Lord Jesus Christ, Son of God, have mercy upon me a sinner.' In repeating this sacred phrase, one is doing more than asking for God's mercy. The Alexandrian Christians felt they were placing their hearts into the heart of God. They learned that one can keep a phrase like this going in one's mind all day long if engaged in manual labor and not needing to interact with others. Saint Paul knew this when he said, 'Pray without ceasing.' (1 Thess. 5:17 KJV)

"Let's stop our busy minds for five minutes and try this form of contemplative prayer. Close your eyes. Relax. Repeat the phrase in time with your breath—either the Greek, 'Kyrie eleison,' or the English, 'Lord, have mercy.' Whenever your mind begins to wander, pull it back to the simplicity of this phrase, reminding yourself that you are in the presence of God."

At the end of the five minutes of silent prayer have one person close with a brief form of *kataphatic* prayer or turn to the Lord's Prayer.

Team Building

Allow three minutes for participants to pair up to talk about thoughts and feelings as they tried this form of prayer. As this type of prayer is not for everyone, allow people to acknowledge that this form of prayer doesn't suit them well.

Debriefing

Once again, ask participants to relate experiences of inviting a friend or family member to worship or making a follow-up call on a parish visitor.

Class Activity

Review and discuss the homework assigned reading.

Quickly turn to the questionnaire to assess your own congregation. Working together, develop a consensus on how your congregation should be rated on each question. Once again, go deeper than merely doing a numerical average of everyone's scores. Try to have each person give reasons why he or she gave the parish a particular rating. Allow forty-five minutes for this part of the exercise.

Once the corporate rating is complete, discuss which of the six stages needs most work in your parish. Develop some goals related to that stage. Then move on to the second weakest stage in your parish. Develop goals to address some of the most glaring needs in that area. Be sure to celebrate some of the things your parish does well in these six stages.

Finally, prioritize the goals that have emerged from this session, so that three or four most important goals are evident as a result of this learning period.

Homework Assignment

Ask participants to read before the next session the "Class Assignment" on pages 107-110.

Closing

The closing prayer can relate to the task of your congregation becoming a more inviting church to the broken, hurting, lonely people in your community who need a church family for support and nurture.

Notes

Goals related to weak areas in new-member assimilation process:

_____

_____

_____

_____

_____

_____

_____

_____

_____

_____

_____

_____

_____

_____

_____

_____

_____

_____

_____

_____

_____

_____

_____

_____

Notes continued . . .

Structuring for Growth

Class Assignment

Before Session 14, read the following article, "Structuring for Growth."

Structuring for Growth

Working with congregations in the years since our study on new member-assimilation, I have become increasingly aware of how many are both structured and staffed for decline. Many congregations are terribly top heavy and bureaucratic. A lot of talented people are involved in running the church, but few are engaged in reaching out to newcomers to help it grow. Many serving on chief decision-making bodies wonder why their church is not growing numerically, yet they are making few decisions that would put energy into such growth.

The behavioral sciences inform us that the most efficient and effective decision-making groups are of a certain size—namely seven plus or minus two. A group larger than twelve has difficulty wrestling with issues and arriving at effective decisions related to those issues. And I continually find boards/councils/vestries/sessions/consistories with more than twelve members. Many have twenty or more members. Recently I worked with a large congregation with forty members on its board. They felt they were a decision-making body, but in fact they were a community of people that reacted to issues rather than dealing with them. What's more, this board wanted to be in on every important decision made in the congregation. With each issue board members enjoyed the opportunity to express views in front of such a large, august body. Yet, by default, decisions in the congregation had to be made elsewhere. Often they were not made.

If I were a power-hungry pastor coming into a congregation, I would appeal to the members that the parish needed to have more people involved in making key decisions. I would recommend that they double the size of their official board. The argument would be hard to resist as it would appeal to members' sense that more people would be involved in the church's operation. Yet the larger the board became, the less able it would be to make effective decisions and the more powerful I would become as, by default, most major decisions would be left up to me. It's a crazy way to make a point, but I hope you get a clear picture of what constitutes an effective decision-making body.

When congregations desire to grow numerically, I often suggest they consider streamlining their organizational structure. Rather than going to all the work of changing constitutions, etc., to provide for such a structural change, I suggest they test out a new structure informally for a year and then decide if they want to make it permanent. I suggest they invite members of their official board, if the number on that board is higher than nine, voluntarily to shift their focus to new-member development and church growth. A core nine could attend ongoing board meetings, while these others focusing on church growth could attend board meetings once a quarter or twice a year. For congregations small in size with limited volunteer resources, this strategy becomes important—if they wish to grow numerically.

In addition to streamlining the structure to free more persons to work on growth effort, I also suggest that the Evangelism Committee (or New-Member Development Committee or New-Member Outreach Committee, or whatever you call it) has a prominent place in the structure; this is not just another committee among others. I have discovered that growing churches give more attention to the work of church growth than any other activity in the church.

The following diagram illustrates the way most congregations structure themselves. The names and number of committees may differ, but most congregations have a hierarchy in which all committees report to the chief decision-making body of the congregation, something like this:

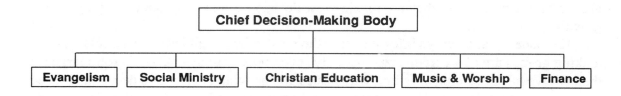

If you really want to grow, I recommend the following structure:

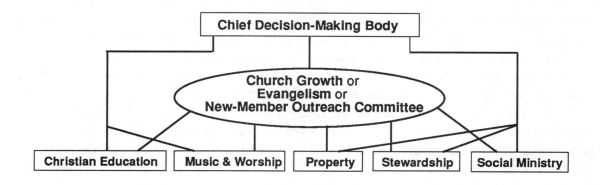

A congregation that really wants to grow needs all systems in the parish gearing up for that effort. The New-Member Outreach Committee needs to be in dialogue with every other committee in the parish, challenging each to focus some energy and attention on the growth issue. The following paragraphs illustrate some creative conversations that might take place between the New-Member Outreach Committee and the other committees of the parish.

New Member Outreach and Christian Education: It is a known fact that children bring their parents to church in that parents, concerned about the spiritual development of their children, seek out quality religious educational experiences.

In what ways could the Sunday school better assure these parents that their children will receive the best religious education available in the community? Is a strategy in place to welcome a parent and child when they walk into your Sunday school for the first time? In what ways might your Sunday school become more attractive to children so they would be motivated to invite their friends to class?

New-Member Outreach and Music and Worship: It is usually at Sunday worship that a congregation first meets a parish visitor, who is not apt to return a second time if that worship service does not provide a quality experience.

How can your parish make it easier for a visitor to enter into the worship experience? How can warmth be expressed to visitors on Sunday morning? If you are a liturgical church, how difficult do you make it for someone not used to liturgical worship to participate? You may know what the "Kyrie" is and where it can be found, but will the parish visitor? How user-friendly is your church bulletin? Do church ushers have a special role in welcoming parish visitors? If so, what training is offered to ushers? How can your congregation effectively gain names and addresses from parish visitors during the Sunday worship experience? What role do parish announcements play in making your congregation a more inviting place? These are but a few of the issues that could be discussed when a New-Member Outreach Committee meets with a Music and Worship Committee to develop a growth strategy for your congregation.

New-Member Outreach and the Property Committee: Appearances are important. What are the first impressions your church building makes on parish visitors? Does the exterior of your church look inviting?

Do you have attractive bulletin boards out in front of the church? To whom are the messages on those signs geared—old timers or parish visitors? A large church in our study was located right next to a four-lane highway leading into a major metropolitan area. We walked around the church twice and could not find any information as to when worship occurred or when Sunday school was held. What a missed opportunity, given this church's location. If you are next to a highway, the sign should face the drivers, not the street. Those traditional signs are meant for horse and buggy days when the driver had time to look sideways and read the church marquee.

What do parish visitors experience as they walk in any outer door of your church?

Do signs direct the parish visitors to key locations in the building? In many of our churches it is easy to get lost, yet it rarely occurs to a Property Committee to look at the building from a visitor's point of view. Here an important conversation can take place between a representative of a New-Member Outreach Committee and a Property Committee member.

New-Member Outreach and Social Ministry: As your Social Ministry Committee faces numerous choices as to how it is going to reach out to the poor, the homeless, the disenfranchised, the hungry, could it simultaneously think in terms of doing some public relations for the congregation?

Congregations located in changing neighborhoods and wanting to reach out to their immediate environments often begin with social ministry activities. Some Social Ministry Committees move out into their neighborhoods and address social need in a concrete way. In this way they not only alleviate suffering, but they also get the attention of the neighborhood by showing that the church cares about the community. If, for example, they discover that the community is experiencing an influx of single parents who have no access to quality day care, establishing a day-care center in the church can become a powerful way of communicating the congregation's care for its neighbors. This is but one example of how social ministry and new-member outreach can work together for effective results.

New-Member Outreach and Stewardship and Finance: Whose responsibility is it to communicate the financial needs of the parish to newcomers? Stewardship or Evangelism? In one of the congregations in our study, this became a heated issue. If Stewardship challenges all members to manage their lives responsibly, when does this effort take over from the effort of getting new members up to par? Are there times when the two efforts need to overlap in bring new members on board? What kind of budget is needed for an effective outreach to newcomers? Does church growth have some priority in the parish budget? What parish budget recommendations could your Evangelism Committee make to make parish growth more possible?

Structuring for growth! Are you beginning to get the picture? Depending on the size of your congregation, it could involve paring down your chief decision-making body to make some key people available to the outreach effort. It could also involve giving the growth effort a more central role in the life of your parish. Do you want to grow numerically? This is unlikely to take place if your growth effort is relegated to some committee that has little impact on other structures in your parish.

Centering

"Let's push ourselves back from the tables. Place anything in your lap on the floor. Align your chest, neck, and head. Place your hands loosely on your thighs, and close your eyes and begin some deep breathing. With every breath, relax your body one more notch.

"Reflect on some day when you felt you were noticeably touched by the Grace of God. Most of us don't want to talk about those times. Was it just our imagination working overtime? Will our friends think us part of the lunatic fringe? Some people are more aware and conscious of those moments than others, yet most of us have them. From time to time it is helpful to recollect those experiences to get an overall sense of our relationship with this great Cosmic Lover.

"As you recollect an experience of Grace, focus on one in which you felt most profoundly aware of the presence of God. What did you feel at the time? What thoughts occurred to you? What did you see? Hear? Smell? Touch? What did you feel as a result of the experience? Did you end up making some resolution—or committing yourself more deeply to some activity? Did you experience some sort of call to change—to do or be something different?

"Return your attention to your breath. What is God calling you to do and be now—in the present? Does God's Grace call you to be an agent of peace or grace to a broken world? Does it call you to the work of helping this church reach out to those who are not grounded in any church family? *(Pause.)* When you are ready, slowly open your eyes."

Team Building

For just five minutes have participants pair up to talk about any sense they had of being called by God to do some piece of work or participate in some activity. What is God calling them to do now? Call them back into plenary session following this brief discussion.

Debriefing

Again ask participants to relate experiences of inviting friends to worship or visiting newcomers.

Class Activity

Summarize and review the assigned reading.

As a group discuss what recommendation for church structure you might like to make to your governing board. Never mind that your group may or may not have much influence with the chief decision-making body. Simply discuss the kind of church structure you feel would best support a growth effort.

Once you are clear about the way you would structure your parish for growth, explore a strategy for getting your governing board to consider experimenting with this new way of operating. Rest assured that they will be attracted to the potential benefit of such a growth effort should you succeed, so you may have more clout with this group than you think.

Once you have a strategy in place, develop a time line and discuss who might write up the recommendations and present them to what critical decision makers. How are you going to support one another in this effort?

Homework Assignment

Announce that there is no assignment for the last session of the workshop.

Closing

In the closing prayer remind yourselves why you are engaged in this effort in the first place—to become more effective agents of healing to a broken world.

Notes

Notes continued . . .

Putting It All Together

Centering

"Close your eyes once again and concentrate on your interior life. As you become aware of your body, identify tension points—your neck, your back, your head. Try to loosen up any tension by breathing deeply, in, out. What feelings are you bringing to this final session? Try to name them. No need to do anything about those feelings, simply note their presence and acknowledge that they will affect your participation in this session.

"Let's move on to an awareness of our feelings about this community that has gathered together for these fifteen sessions. How have your perceptions of the group changed since the first time we met? Remember our first session? We discussed how comfortable—or uncomfortable—we were in verbalizing our Christian faith. (Have participants take some time to track the evolution of their perceptions of the group up until this final session. Remind them of various memorable incidents. As feelings about groups and individuals are generally mixed, have people focus on negative as well as positive feelings.

"Psalm 68:6 says that God places the solitary into families. Why might God do this? How is that part of the Grace and Mercy of God?"

Have someone read Romans 12:1-10. Offer a prayer, focusing on the richness you all enjoy given the kind of community your church provides you. Ask for God's help in making your parish a place to which those out there in the world without a caring community will come to drink from the same cup that you all share.

Debriefing

Set aside no more than fifteen minutes for individuals to relate stories of having either invited a friend to worship or completed a follow-up visit to a parish visitor.

Class Activity

In this final session you want to pull together and prioritize the insights, learnings, and goals from previous sessions. It is also time to have group participants assess their level of commitment to continued work in new-member ministries.

Prioritizing Insights and Goals

Work together to review your insights and goal statements from selected sessions and place them before you on one single list. On newsprint have someone list in goal language the desires of the group for your congregation. Using the following guidelines and review of selected sessions, your newsprint notes from these sessions, and participants' workbook notes, list your top-priority goals for each ministry area. Basically these are things you would like to change, get started, or accentuate to help your congregation become a more inviting church. List goals from these sessions:

Session 2: Do you have goals related to congregational size and your desire to move from one size to another? Place these on the list.

Session 4: Growing out of your interviews with newcomers to your parish, what would you like to change or amend about the way your congregation brings on board new members? Place these changes on the list in goal language.

Session 5: In this session on historical reflection you developed and prioritized meaning statements. In goal language place these meaning statements on the list. Include some goals that capitalize on your congregation's strengths and some that minimize or change negative dimensions of the parish.

Session 6: Recall the evening you spent on parish norms, the unwritten rules by which you live in the parish. Which of these would you like to change? Which do you wish to highlight because they are key strengths of the parish? In goal language, place these on the list.

Session 7: In this session you completed a questionnaire on which you rated types of people by three categories, Top—Middle—Bottom, depending on how welcome they are in your church. Did insights emerge from this session that you can put into goal language and place on this list?

Session 8: Recall talking about being more inviting to children. Are there children's ministry goals that you wish to place on this list?

Session 10: In this session you explored doing follow-up visits to parish visitors. Are there goals for the parish that you would like to place on this list as a result of this discussion and subsequent home visits?

Session 11: Recall your discussion on the requirements for church membership. Did you agree on ways you might deepen the meaning of membership by developing some challenges for both your core leadership in the parish and your new members? If so, do you wish to place any of these goals on the list?

Session 12: Are there goals that emerged from your group related to how you might better manage the volunteer energies within your parish? What pathways for spiritual growth would benefit your newcomers and members? Place any goals from this session on your list.

Session 13: In goal language, what emerged from your analysis of your parish's new-member assimilation process?

Session 14: Did you reach structure conclusions related to how you might like to streamline your parish for a greater emphasis on church growth? If so, place these goals on your list.

At this point you have accumulated a long list of things you would like to change or accomplish to make your parish more inviting. It will be impossible for you to do all these things in the next several years. Use the following process to surface the changes your group feels are most urgent or most vital to your becoming a more welcoming place.

Step 1: This list needs to be pared down to no more than twelve or fifteen goals. You may want to take a quick vote to determine which should be the twelve or fifteen priority goals. Number these top twelve or fifteen goals and have them in view of everyone.

Step 2: Have everyone tear up a sheet of paper into either twelve or fifteen strips, depending on the number of goals in your short list. On each slip of paper have them write out one of the twelve/fifteen goals along with its corresponding number.

Step 3: Once they have written out these goals, one on each separate piece of paper, have them take a few minutes to go off by themselves and place these goals in three separate piles—TOP—MIDDLE—BOTTOM (with an equal number of goals in each pile). The TOP category is for goals rated most important. The BOTTOM category is for goals rated low-priority. After they have sorted goals into three piles, have them mark *each goal* with a T, M, or B. Once all the separate sheets have been marked by category, participants should return all the goals in a numerical order.
    Now comes the fun!

Step 4: Divide the room into three separate stations with the words TOP, MIDDLE, and BOTTOM posted by each station. Call out "goal number one" and have the participants walk to the station representing their ranking of that goal. With each goal, as people move physically to a station, they will see how everyone else has ranked that goal. This allows a quick debate about the relative value of that goal to the overall objective of helping your congregation become a more inviting church. Allow no more than three minutes for people to try to convince others standing at another station that they ought to change their votes. *Ground Rule* in this exercise: Persons can change their minds on their rating of a goal, but if they do so they will need to shift another rating on their whole list so that they still end up with equal numbers in each of the three categories. For example, someone may convince you that you need to give a certain goal a TOP priority. But when you switch, you will need to move one of your other TOP priorities into a MIDDLE or BOTTOM category.

After a three-minute debate, say, "Has anyone changed a vote on this goal?" Count how many people are standing at each of the three stations. Mark the count on newsprint, and then say, "Goal number two." Continue this process through all twelve or fifteen goals.

Step 5: With a simple mathematical calculation, you can surface the top five goals of the group. Simply multiply all the TOP votes by three, all the MIDDLE votes by two, and the BOTTOM votes by one. Add up the total for the numerical rating of that goal. Then choose the five that have the highest ratings. Take a few minutes now to have people express their feelings about the five top goals that have emerged. Ask if these five feel right to them. Can they support these as the goals that need to have priority for the next twelve months? Retain all the remaining goals. Some are short-term goals (in any ranking) that can be easily met, allowing you to concentrate on long-term goals.

Personal Objectives

Devote the last fifteen minutes of the session to having each individual assess his or her continued role in new-member ministry. If the initial agreement at the front end of the course was that after fifteen sessions individuals could decide whether or not they wanted to continue to serve on an outreach group, that decision needs to be honored.

This is a good time to have participants express their commitment to further work; they can now see clearly which goals are recommended as having priority in the next twelve months. Do they want to work to make some of them a reality?

Give each participant a couple of minutes to express any personal affinity with these goals or with efforts that have been tested in this seminar, such as follow-up visits to parish visitors. How do they see their continued role in this effort? Respect the desires of people who claim they appreciated the course but simply do not have the time for ongoing work.

If the group is an already established committee of the church, ask participants if they wish to work on any one of the five goals just highlighted. I would recommend establishing a separate task force for each goal. The task force could include members of the parish not on this committee. A small church will need only three or four people working on the development of each goal. Ask committee members whether or not they would like to head up a task force.

If the group does not have authority to work on the goals, go around the room having participants identify any high-priority goals to which they would like to offer energy and commitment. Discuss how these people can and should express their interest, ideas, and concerns to the appropriate authority-bearing group. Identify channels and strategies.

Neither good ideas nor energy for follow-through should be lost at this point. This workshop could be a turning point for your congregation. People who have caught the vision need to make sure these ideas become part of the congregation's life.

On the other hand, remind participants that church leaders may or may not be receptive to ideas and suggestions made in these sessions. Church committees may welcome the work of this committee like springtime; then again they may not. Even if no official action comes from these sessions, those of you involved have received incredible value from them.

You've learned how to be a more welcoming individual. You've learned how to reach out with warmth. You've learned something about and from the history of this parish. Through the centering and team-building exercises you've gotten to know yourselves and other church members more intimately. Ask the group for other valuable lessons they've learned personally from this workshop. Again, even if no church committee catches the vision for and implements goals presented here, the workshop itself has improved the community life of the church. Praise God for that.

Whether or not your group is an ongoing committee, have members take a minute to express their personal learnings from the course. How has their behavior changed as a result of any experiences in these fifteen sessions? Sometimes what we learn becomes part of our lives only as we verbalize it to friends and associates.

Before you close, ask someone to read aloud the following "Class Reading."

Class Reading: A Note from the Author

My personal best wishes to you as a group and as a congregation. As I travel around the country doing workshops on new-member outreach, I am encouraged by the creativity and commitment of people who want their churches to thrive and grow, despite obstacles presented in this day and age. Be aware that your efforts on your church's behalf are joined with millions of other Christians who are working to keep the Gospel message of the church alive.

God's peace and blessing to each of you personally.

Roy M. Oswald

Closing

The closing prayer can express thanksgiving for this time with others and the personal insights gained. Closing petitions could be that everyone find continued strength and courage to be a more inviting person on behalf of the congregation and that the congregation as a whole receive guidance to become a warmer place for the broken, lonely, and despairing to enter.

Notes

Top priority goals:

_____

_____

_____

_____

_____

_____

_____

_____

_____

_____

_____

_____

_____

_____

_____

_____

_____

_____

_____

_____

_____

_____

_____

_____

_____

_____

_____

Notes continued . . .

Notes continued . . .

Notes continued . . .

Notes continued . . .

Notes continued . . .

Notes continued . . .

Notes continued . . .

Notes continued . . .

Notes continued . . .

Notes continued . . .

Notes continued . . .

The Alban Institute:
an invitation to membership

The Alban Institute, begun in 1979, believes that the congregation is essential to the task of equipping the people of God to minister in the church and the world. A multi-denominational membership organization, the Institute provides on-site training, educational programs, consulting, research, and publishing for hundreds of churches across the country.

The Alban Institute invites you to be a member of this partnership of laity, clergy, and executives—a partnership that brings together people who are raising important questions about congregational life and people who are trying new solutions, making new discoveries, finding a new way of getting clear about the task of ministry. The Institute exists to provide you with the kinds of information and resources you need to support your ministries.

Join us now and enjoy these benefits:

Action Information, a highly respected journal published six times a year, to keep you up to date on current issues and trends.

Inside Information, Alban's quarterly newsletter, keeps you informed about research and other happenings around Alban. Available to members only.

Publications Discounts:

- ☐ 15% for Individual, Retired Clergy, and Seminarian Members
- ☐ 25% for Congregational Members
- ☐ 40% for Judicatory and Seminary Executive Members

Discounts on Training and Education Events

Write our Membership Department at the address below or call us at (202) 244-7320 for more information about how to join The Alban Institute's growing membership, particularly about Congregational Membership in which 12 designated persons receive all benefits of membership.

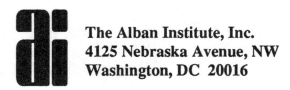

The Alban Institute, Inc.
4125 Nebraska Avenue, NW
Washington, DC 20016